Presented to

_____

By

_____

On the Occasion of

_____

Date

_____

GOD'S PROMISES *for* YOU

THE BIBLE
PROMISE BOOK

NEW LIFE VERSION

BARBOUR

© 2006 by Barbour Publishing, Inc.

ISBN 978-1-59789-679-5

All scripture is taken from the HOLY BIBLE, New Life Version, copyright © 1969–2003 by Christian Literature International, P.O. Box 777, Canby, OR 97013. Used by permission.

Wherever * is seen, the words that follow are not in all the early writings of the New Testament. If part of a verse or more than one verse is missing in some of the early writings, it is marked [*].

Cover design by Studio Gearbox: www.studiogearbox.com

Published by Barbour Publishing, Inc., P.O. Box 719, Uhrichsville, Ohio 44683, www.barbourbooks.com

Our mission is to publish and distribute inspirational products offering exceptional value and biblical encouragement to the masses.

Member of the
Evangelical Christian
Publishers Association

Printed in China.
5 4 3 2

Contents

Anger. 7
Charity 10
Children 14
Children's Duties 16
Comfort. 18
Contentment. 21
Correction, God's 22
Courage. 23
Death. 25
Enemies. 28
Eternal Life 32
Faith 37
Faithfulness, God's. 40
Fear 43
Food and Clothing 48
Forgiveness 49
Fruitfulness. 51
Gossip. 53
Grace, Growth in. 54
Guidance 57
Guilt 59
Help in Troubles 61
Holy Spirit. 65
Honesty 68
Hope. 71
Hospitality. 72
Humility 75
Jealousy. 77
Joy 80
Laziness 83
Loneliness 86
Long Life 87

Love, Brotherly 89
Love, God's 91
Loving God 95
Lust 97
Lying 101
Marriage 104
Mercy 106
Money 108
Obedience 112
Parents' Duties 115
Patience 117
Peace 119
Poverty 120
Prayer 122
Pride 126
Prisoners 128
Protection, God's 129
Repentance 132
Righteousness 133
Salvation 136
Seeking God 138
Self-Denial 140
Self-Righteousness 142
Sexual Sins 144
Shame 147
Sickness 148
Sin, Freedom from 150
Sin, Redemption from 151
Slander and Reproach 154
Success 155
Trust 159
Wisdom 162
Word of God 164
Work 168
Worry 171
Worship 174

ANGER

The Lord is full of loving-favor and pity, slow to anger and great in loving-kindness.

PSALM 145:8

"You are a forgiving God. You are kind and loving, slow to anger, and full of loving-kindness."

NEHEMIAH 9:17

For His anger lasts only a short time. But His favor is for life. Crying may last for a night, but joy comes with the new day.

PSALM 30:5

My Christian brothers, you know everyone should listen much and speak little. He should be slow to become angry. A man's anger does not allow him to be right with God.

JAMES 1:19-20

Do not be quick in spirit to be angry. For anger is in the heart of fools.

ECCLESIASTES 7:9

He who has a quick temper acts in a foolish way, and a man who makes sinful plans is hated.

PROVERBS 14:17

He who is slow to anger is better than the powerful. And he who rules his spirit is better than he who takes a city.

PROVERBS 16:32

A man with a bad temper starts fights, but he who is slow to anger quiets fighting.

PROVERBS 15:18

A man of anger starts fights, and a man with a bad temper is full of wrong-doing.

PROVERBS 29:22

Stop being angry. Turn away from fighting. Do not trouble yourself. It leads only to wrong-doing.

PSALM 37:8

Do not have anything to do with a man given to anger, or go with a man who has a bad temper. Or you might learn his ways and get yourself into a trap.

PROVERBS 22:24—25

A gentle answer turns away anger, but a sharp word causes anger.

PROVERBS 15:1

If you are angry, do not let it become sin. Get over your anger before the day is finished.

EPHESIANS 4:26

A man's understanding makes him slow to anger. It is to his honor to forgive and forget a wrong done to him.

PROVERBS 19:11

"But I tell you that whoever is angry with his brother will be guilty and have to suffer for his wrong-doing."

MATTHEW 5:22

Put out of your life all these things: bad feelings about other people, anger, temper, loud talk, bad talk which hurts other people, and bad feelings which hurt other people. You must be kind to each other. Think of the other person. Forgive other people just as God forgave you because of Christ's death on the cross.

EPHESIANS 4:31–32

Put out of your life these things also: anger, bad temper, bad feelings toward others, talk that hurts people, speaking against God, and dirty talk.

COLOSSIANS 3:8

CHARITY

Happy is the man who cares for the poor. The Lord will save him in times of trouble. The Lord will keep him alive and safe. And he will be happy upon the earth. You will not give him over to the desire of those who hate him.

PSALM 41:1–2

He who shows kindness to a poor man gives to the Lord and He will pay him in return for his good act.

PROVERBS 19:17

"When you have a supper, ask poor people. Ask those who cannot walk and those who are blind. You will be happy if you do this. They cannot pay you back. You will get your reward when the people who are right with God are raised from the dead."

LUKE 14:13–14

"Sell what you have and give the money to poor people. Have money-bags for yourselves that will never wear out. These money-bags are riches in heaven that will always be there. No robber can take them and no bugs can eat them there."

LUKE 12:33

He who hates his neighbor sins, but happy is he who shows loving-favor to the poor.

PROVERBS 14:21

He has given much to the poor. His right-standing with God lasts forever. His horn will be lifted high in honor.

PSALM 112:9

He who gives much will be honored, for he gives some of his food to the poor.

PROVERBS 22:9

"Give, and it will be given to you. You will have more than enough. It can be pushed down and shaken together and it will still run over as it is given to you. The way you give to others is the way you will receive in return."

LUKE 6:38

He who gives to the poor will never want, but many bad things will happen to the man who shuts his eyes to the poor.

PROVERBS 28:27

Each man should give as he has decided in his heart. He should not give, wishing he could keep it. Or he should not give if he feels he has to give. God loves a man who gives because he wants to give.

2 CORINTHIANS 9:7

There is one who is free in giving, and yet he grows richer. And there is one who keeps what he should give, but he ends up needing more. The man who gives much will have much, and he who helps others will be helped himself.

PROVERBS 11:24–25

I have been young, and now I am old. Yet I have never seen the man who is right with God left alone, or his children begging for bread. All day long he is kind and lets others use what he has. And his children make him happy.

PSALM 37:25–26

"If you give what you have to the hungry, and fill the needs of those who suffer, then your light will rise in the darkness, and your darkness will be like the brightest time of day."

ISAIAH 58:10

Tell those who are rich in this world not to be proud and not to trust in their money. Money cannot be trusted. They should put their trust in God.

He gives us all we need for our happiness. Tell them to do good and be rich in good works. They should give much to those in need and be ready to share.

1 TIMOTHY 6:17–18

"Is it not a time to share your food with the hungry, and bring the poor man into your house who has no home of his own? Is it not a time to give clothes to the person you see who has no clothes, and a time not to hide yourself from your own family? Then your light will break out like the early morning, and you will soon be healed. Your right and good works will go before you. And the shining-greatness of the Lord will keep watch behind you."

ISAIAH 58:7–8

"And the Levite who has no share of what is given to you, and the stranger, and the child without parents, and the woman whose husband has died, who are in your towns, may come and eat and be filled. Then the Lord your God will bring good to you in all the work done by your hands."

DEUTERONOMY 14:29

Jesus looked at him with love and said, "There is one thing for you to do yet. Go and sell everything you have and give the money to poor people. You will have riches in heaven. Then come and follow Me."

MARK 10:21

CHILDREN

"Put your trust in the Lord Jesus Christ and you and your family will be saved from the punishment of sin."

ACTS 16:31

"This promise is to you and your children. It is to all people everywhere. It is to as many as the Lord our God will call."

ACTS 2:39

"All your sons will be taught by the Lord, and the well-being of your children will be great."

ISAIAH 54:13

"For I will pour water on the thirsty land and rivers on the dry ground. I will pour out My Spirit on your children, and will bring good to your children's children."

ISAIAH 44:3

"Let the little children come to Me. Do not stop them. The holy nation of God is made up of ones like these. For sure, I tell you, whoever does not receive the holy nation of God as a little child does not go into it." He took the children in His arms. He put His hands on them and prayed that good would come to them.

MARK 10:14–16

See, children are a gift from the Lord. The children born to us are our special pay. The children of a young man are like arrows in the hand of a soldier. Happy is the man who has many of them. They will not be put to shame when they speak in the gate with those who hate them.

PSALM 127:3–5

Your wife will be like a vine with much fruit within your house. Your children will be like olive plants around your table.

PSALM 128:3

But He lifts those in need out of their troubles. He makes their families grow like flocks.

PSALM 107:41

Grandchildren are the pride and joy of old men and a son is proud of his father.

PROVERBS 17:6

CHILDREN'S DUTIES

Children, as Christians, obey your parents. This is the right thing to do. Respect your father and mother. This is the first Law given that had a promise. The promise is this: If you respect your father and mother, you will live a long time and your life will be full of many good things.

EPHESIANS 6:1–3

Children, obey your parents in everything. The Lord is pleased when you do.

COLOSSIANS 3:20

"Respect your father and your mother."

LUKE 18:20

"Cursed is the one who puts his father or mother to shame."

DEUTERONOMY 27:16

"Every one of you must have respect for his mother and his father."

LEVITICUS 19:3

"Honor your father and your mother, as the Lord your God has told you."

DEUTERONOMY 5:16

My son, keep the teaching of your father, and do not turn away from the teaching of your mother.

PROVERBS 6:20

A wise son listens when his father tells him the right way, but one who laughs at the truth does not listen when strong words are spoken to him.

PROVERBS 13:1

A fool turns away from the strong teaching of his father, but he who remembers the strong words spoken to him is wise.

PROVERBS 15:5

A young man makes himself known by his actions and proves if his ways are pure and right.

PROVERBS 20:11

A wise son makes a father glad, but a foolish son is a sorrow to his mother.

PROVERBS 10:1

Listen to your father who gave you life, and do not hate your mother when she is old.

PROVERBS 23:22

The father of one who is right with God will have much joy. He who has a wise son will be glad in him. Let your father and mother be glad, and let her who gave birth to you be full of joy. Give me your heart, my son. Let your eyes find joy in my ways.

PROVERBS 23:24–26

COMFORT

God is our safe place and our strength. He is always our help when we are in trouble. So we will not be afraid, even if the earth is shaken and the mountains fall into the center of the sea, and even if its waters go wild with storm and the mountains shake with its action.

PSALM 46:1–3

Even if I walk into trouble, You will keep my life safe. You will put out Your hand against the anger of those who hate me. And Your right hand will save me.

PSALM 138:7

The Lord is my rock, and my safe place, and the One Who takes me out of trouble. My God is my rock, in Whom I am safe. He is my safe-covering, my saving strength, and my strong tower.

PSALM 18:2

For He has not turned away from the suffering of the one in pain or trouble. He has not hidden His face from him. But He has heard his cry for help.

PSALM 22:24

When he falls, he will not be thrown down, because the Lord holds his hand.

PSALM 37:24

The Lord is good, a safe place in times of trouble. And He knows those who come to Him to be safe.

NAHUM 1:7

But the saving of those who are right with God is from the Lord. He is their strength in time of trouble.

PSALM 37:39

Give all your cares to the Lord and He will give you strength. He will never let those who are right with Him be shaken.

PSALM 55:22

"I have told you these things so you may have peace in Me. In the world you will have much trouble. But take hope! I have power over the world!"

JOHN 16:33

"Come to Me, all of you who work and have heavy loads. I will give you rest."

MATTHEW 11:28

As we have suffered much for Christ and have shared in His pain, we also share His great comfort.

2 CORINTHIANS 1:5

The Lord also keeps safe those who suffer. He is a safe place in times of trouble.

PSALM 9:9

For the Lord will not turn away from a man forever. For if He causes sorrow, He will have loving-pity because of His great loving-kindness. He does not want to cause trouble or sorrow for the children of men.

LAMENTATIONS 3:31–33

Wait for the Lord. Be strong. Let your heart be strong. Yes, wait for the Lord.

PSALM 27:14

CONTENTMENT

A glad heart is good medicine, but a broken spirit dries up the bones.

PROVERBS 17:22

Keep your lives free from the love of money. Be happy with what you have. God has said, "I will never leave you or let you be alone."(Deuteronomy 31:6)

HEBREWS 13:5

All the days of the suffering are hard, but a glad heart has a special supper all the time.

PROVERBS 15:15

A heart that has peace is life to the body, but wrong desires are like the wasting away of the bones.

PROVERBS 14:30

A God-like life gives us much when we are happy for what we have.

1 TIMOTHY 6:6

Do not let your heart be jealous of sinners, but live in the fear of the Lord always. For sure there is a future and your hope will not be cut off.

PROVERBS 23:17–18

CORRECTION, GOD'S

The Lord punishes everyone He loves. He whips every son He receives.

PROVERBS 3:12

"See, happy is the man to whom God speaks strong words. So do not hate the strong teaching of the All-powerful. He punishes, but He gives comfort. He hurts, but His hands heal."

JOB 5:17–18

Happy is the man who is punished until he gives up sin, O Lord, and whom You teach from Your Law. You give him rest from days of trouble, until a hole is dug for the sinful.

PSALM 94:12–13

This is the reason we do not give up. Our human body is wearing out. But our spirits are getting stronger every day. The little troubles we suffer now for a short time are making us ready for the great things God is going to give us forever.

2 CORINTHIANS 4:16—17

For a little while our fathers on earth punished us when they thought they should. But God punishes us for our good so we will be holy as He is holy. There is no joy while we are being punished. It is hard to take, but later we can see that good came from it. And it gives us the peace of being right with God.

HEBREWS 12:10—11

COURAGE

Wait for the Lord. Be strong. Let your heart be strong. Yes, wait for the Lord.

PSALM 27:14

For the Lord loves what is fair and right. He does not leave the people alone who belong to Him. They are kept forever. But the children of the sinful will be cut off.

PSALM 37:28

But now the Lord Who made you, O Jacob, and He Who made you, O Israel, says, "Do not be afraid. For I have bought you and made you free. I have called you by name. You are Mine!"

ISAIAH 43:1

Trust in the Lord, and do good. So you will live in the land and will be fed.

PSALM 37:3

He gives strength to the weak. And He gives power to him who has little strength.

ISAIAH 40:29

Be strong. Be strong in heart, all you who hope in the Lord.

PSALM 31:24

I know how to get along with little and how to live when I have much. I have learned the secret of being happy at all times. If I am full of food and have all I need, I am happy. If I am hungry and need more, I am happy. I can do all things because Christ gives me the strength.

PHILIPPIANS 4:12–13

"Have I not told you? Be strong and have strength of heart! Do not be afraid or lose faith. For the Lord your God is with you anywhere you go."

JOSHUA 1:9

Watch and keep awake! Stand true to the Lord. Keep on acting like men and be strong.

1 CORINTHIANS 16:13

DEATH

Yes, even if I walk through the valley of the shadow of death, I will not be afraid of anything, because You are with me. You have a walking stick with which to guide and one with which to help. These comfort me.

PSALM 23:4

O death, where is your power? O death, where are your pains?

1 CORINTHIANS 15:55

The sinful is thrown down by his wrong-doing, but the man who is right with God has a safe place when he dies.

PROVERBS 14:32

Now that we have been saved from the punishment of sin by the blood of Christ, He will save us from God's anger also.

ROMANS 5:9

It is true that we share the same Father with Jesus. And it is true that we share the same kind of flesh and blood because Jesus became a man like us. He died as we must die. Through His death He destroyed the power of the devil who has the power of death.

HEBREWS 2:14–15

"For sure, I tell you, if anyone keeps My Word, that one will never die."

JOHN 8:51

This is God, our God forever and ever. He will show us the way until death.

PSALM 48:14

My body and my heart may grow weak, but God is the strength of my heart and all I need forever.

PSALM 73:26

But God will free my soul from the power of the grave. For He will take me to Himself.

PSALM 49:15

He will take away death for all time. The Lord God will dry tears from all faces.

ISAIAH 25:8

"I will pay the price to free them from the power of the grave. I will save them from death. O Death, where are your thorns? O Grave, where is your power to destroy? I will have no loving-pity."

HOSEA 13:14

Look at the man without blame. And watch the man who is right and good. For the man of peace will have much family to follow him.

PSALM 37:37

This is the reason we do not give up. Our human body is wearing out. But our spirits are getting stronger every day.

2 CORINTHIANS 4:16

For I know that nothing can keep us from the love of God. Death cannot! Life cannot! Angels cannot! Leaders cannot! Any other power cannot! Hard things now or in the future cannot! The world above or the world below cannot! Any other living thing cannot keep us away from the love of God which is ours through Christ Jesus our Lord.

ROMANS 8:38–39

ENEMIES

The Lord helps them and takes them out of trouble. He takes them away from the sinful, and saves them, because they go to Him for a safe place.

PSALM 37:40

"Those who hate you will be dressed with shame. And the tent of the sinful will be no more."

JOB 8:22

"The Lord will cause you to win the battles against those who fight against you. They will come against you one way, and run away from you seven ways."

DEUTERONOMY 28:7

"For the Lord your God is the One Who goes with you. He will fight for you against those who hate you. And He will save you."

DEUTERONOMY 20:4

"He will keep you from death in times of no food, and from the power of the sword in war."

JOB 5:20

With God's help we will do well. And He will break under His feet those who fight against us.

PSALM 60:12

"No tool that is made to fight against you will do well. And you will prove wrong every tongue that says you are guilty. This is the gift given to the servants of the Lord. I take away their guilt and make them right," says the Lord.

ISAIAH 54:17

The Lord is with me. He is my Helper. I will watch those lose who fight against me.

PSALM 118:7

"He promised that we would be saved from those who hate us and that we might worship Him without being afraid."

LUKE 1:74

For the sinful will not rule over the land of those who are right with God. So those who are right and good may not use their hands to do wrong.

PSALM 125:3

For in the day of trouble He will keep me safe in His holy tent. In the secret place of His tent He will hide me. He will set me high upon a rock. Then my head will be lifted up above all those around me who hate me. I will give gifts in His holy tent with a loud voice of joy. I will sing. Yes, I will sing praises to the Lord.

PSALM 27:5–6

When the ways of a man are pleasing to the Lord, He makes even those who hate him to be at peace with him.

PROVERBS 16:7

"Will not God make the things that are right come to His chosen people who cry day and night to Him? Will He wait a long time to help them?"

LUKE 18:7

"If anyone brings trouble against you, it will not be from Me. Whoever comes against you will fall because of you."

ISAIAH 54:15

Let those who love the Lord hate what is bad. For He keeps safe the souls of His faithful ones. He takes them away from the hand of the sinful.

PSALM 97:10

"I will save you on that day," says the Lord. "You will not be given over to the men you are afraid of. For I will be sure to take you away, and you will not be killed by the sword. You will have your life because you have trusted in Me," says the Lord.

JEREMIAH 39:17–18

"Fear the Lord your God and He will save you from those who hate you."

2 KINGS 17:39

He answered, "Do not be afraid. For those who are with us are more than those who are with them."

2 KINGS 6:16

Do not be afraid of fear that comes all at once. And do not be afraid of the storm of the sinful when it comes. For the Lord will be your trust. He will keep your foot from being caught.

PROVERBS 3:25–26

"See, all those who are angry with you will be put to shame and troubled. Those who fight against you will be as nothing and will be lost. You will look for those who argue with you, but will not find them. Those who war against you will be as nothing, as nothing at all."

ISAIAH 41:11–12

So we can say for sure, "The Lord is my Helper. I am not afraid of anything man can do to me." (Psalm 118:6)

HEBREWS 13:6

ETERNAL LIFE

"For sure, I tell you, he who puts his trust in Me has life that lasts forever."

JOHN 6:47

Jesus said to her, "I am the One Who raises the dead and gives them life. Anyone who puts his trust in Me will live again, even if he dies. Anyone who lives and has put his trust in Me will never die. Do you believe this?"

JOHN 11:25–26

For sure, I am telling you a secret. We will not all die, but we will all be changed. In a very short time, no longer than it takes for the eye to close and open, the Christians who have died will be raised. It will happen when the last horn sounds. The dead will be raised never to die again. Then the rest of us who are alive will be changed. Our human bodies made from dust must be changed into a body that cannot be destroyed. Our human bodies that can die must be changed into bodies that will never die. When this that can be destroyed has been changed into that which cannot be destroyed, and when this that does die has been changed into that which cannot die, then it will happen as the Holy Writings said it would happen. They said, "Death has no more power over life." (Isaiah 25:8)

1 CORINTHIANS 15:51–54

And He has promised us life that lasts forever!

1 JOHN 2:25

Death came because of a man, Adam. Being raised from the dead also came because of a Man, Christ.

1 CORINTHIANS 15:21

I have written these things to you who believe in the name of the Son of God. Now you can know you have life that lasts forever.

1 JOHN 5:13

"Do not be surprised at this. The time is coming when all who are in their graves will hear His voice. They will come out. Those who have done good will be raised again and will have new life. Those who have been sinful will be raised again and will be told they are guilty and will be punished."

JOHN 5:28–29

For the Lord Himself will come down from heaven with a loud call. The head angel will speak with a loud voice. God's horn will give its sounds. First, those who belong to Christ will come out of their graves to meet the Lord. Then those of us who are still living here on earth will be gathered together with them in the clouds. We will meet the Lord in the sky and be with Him forever.

1 THESSALONIANS 4:16–17

"For God so loved the world that He gave His only Son. Whoever puts his trust in God's Son will not be lost but will have life that lasts forever."

JOHN 3:16

It is the same with people who are raised from the dead. The body will turn back to dust when it is put in a grave. When the body is raised from the grave, it will never die. It has no greatness when it is put in a grave, but it is raised with shining-greatness. It is weak when it is put in a grave, but it is raised with power. It is a human body when it dies, but it is a God-like body when it is raised from the dead. There are human bodies and there are God-like bodies. The Holy Writings say, "The first man, Adam, became a living soul." But the last Adam (Christ) is a life-giving Spirit. We have these human bodies first. Then we are given God-like bodies that are ready for heaven.

1 CORINTHIANS 15:42–46

The Holy Spirit raised Jesus from the dead. If the same Holy Spirit lives in you, He will give life to your bodies in the same way.

ROMANS 8:11

"God will take away all their tears. There will be no more death or sorrow or crying or pain. All the old things have passed away."

REVELATION 21:4

You get what is coming to you when you sin. It is death! But God's free gift is life that lasts forever. It is given to us by our Lord Jesus Christ.

ROMANS 6:23

If a man does things to please his sinful old self, his soul will be lost. If a man does things to please the Holy Spirit, he will have life that lasts forever.

GALATIANS 6:8

"Many of those who sleep in the dust of the earth will wake up. Some will have life that lasts forever, but others will have shame and will suffer much forever."

DANIEL 12:2

For You will not give me over to the grave. And You will not allow Your Holy One to return to dust.

PSALM 16:10

We know about it now because of the coming of Jesus Christ, the One Who saves. He put a stop to the power of death and brought life that never dies which is seen through the Good News.

2 TIMOTHY 1:10

This is the word He spoke: God gave us life that lasts forever, and this life is in His Son.

1 JOHN 5:11

Our body is like a house we live in here on earth. When it is destroyed, we know that God has another body for us in heaven. The new one will not be made by human hands as a house is made. This body will last forever.

2 CORINTHIANS 5:1

"There are many rooms in My Father's house. If it were not so, I would have told you. I am going away to make a place for you. After I go and make a place for you, I will come back and take you with Me. Then you may be where I am."

JOHN 14:2–3

"The Father sent Me. He did not want Me to lose any of all those He gave Me. He wants Me to raise them to life on the last day. He wants everyone who sees the Son to put his trust in Him and have life that lasts forever. I will raise that one up on the last day."

JOHN 6:39–40

"But those who have the right to have that life and are raised from the dead do not marry and are not given in marriage. They cannot die anymore. They are as the angels and are sons of God. They are children who have been raised from the dead."

LUKE 20:35–36

"My sheep hear My voice and I know them. They follow Me. I give them life that lasts forever. They will never be punished. No one is able to take them out of My hand."

JOHN 10:27–28

"Whoever eats My flesh and drinks My blood has life that lasts forever. I will raise him up on the last day."

JOHN 6:54

FAITH

Now faith is being sure we will get what we hope for. It is being sure of what we cannot see.

HEBREWS 11:1

A man cannot please God unless he has faith. Anyone who comes to God must believe that He is. That one must also know that God gives what is promised to the one who keeps on looking for Him.

HEBREWS 11:6

If you do not have wisdom, ask God for it. He is always ready to give it to you and will never say you are wrong for asking. You must have faith as you ask Him. You must not doubt. Anyone who doubts is like a wave which is pushed around by the sea.

JAMES 1:5–6

As you have put your trust in Christ Jesus the Lord to save you from the punishment of sin, now let Him lead you in every step. Have your roots planted deep in Christ. Grow in Him. Get your strength from Him. Let Him make you strong in the faith as you have been taught. Your life should be full of thanks to Him.

COLOSSIANS 2:6–7

For by His loving-favor you have been saved from the punishment of sin through faith. It is not by anything you have done. It is a gift of God.

EPHESIANS 2:8

But the fruit that comes from having the Holy Spirit in our lives is: love, joy, peace, not giving up, being kind, being good, having faith, being gentle, and being the boss over our own desires.

GALATIANS 5:22–23

I have been put up on the cross to die with Christ. I no longer live. Christ lives in me. The life I now live in this body, I live by putting my trust in the Son of God. He was the One Who loved me and gave Himself for me.

GALATIANS 2:20

Jesus said to them, "Have faith in God. For sure, I tell you, a person may say to this mountain, 'Move from here into the sea.' And if he does not doubt, but believes that what he says will be done, it will happen."

MARK 11:22–23

I pray that Christ may live in your hearts by faith. I pray that you will be filled with love. I pray that you will be able to understand how wide and how long and how high and how deep His love is. I pray that you will know the love of Christ. His love goes beyond anything we can understand. I pray that you will be filled with God Himself.

EPHESIANS 3:17–19

All these many people who have had faith in God are around us like a cloud. Let us put every thing out of our lives that keeps us from doing what we should. Let us keep running in the race that God has planned for us. Let us keep looking to Jesus. Our faith comes from Him and He is the One Who makes it perfect. He did not give up when He had to suffer shame and die on a cross. He knew of the joy that would be His later. Now He is sitting at the right side of God.

HEBREWS 12:1–2

"The one who has faith can do all things."

MARK 9:23

Jesus said to him, "Thomas, because you have seen Me, you believe. Those are happy who have never seen Me and yet believe!"

JOHN 20:29

FAITHFULNESS, GOD'S

"Know then that the Lord your God is God, the faithful God. He keeps His promise and shows His loving-kindness to those who love Him and keep His Laws, even to a thousand family groups in the future."

DEUTERONOMY 7:9

"For the Lord your God is a God of loving-pity. He will not leave you or destroy you or forget the agreement He promised to your fathers."

DEUTERONOMY 4:31

He has remembered His agreement forever, the promise He made to last through a thousand families-to-come.

PSALM 105:8

"God is not a man, that He should lie. He is not a son of man, that he should be sorry for what He has said. Has He said, and will He not do it? Has He spoken, and will He not keep His Word?"

NUMBERS 23:19

Let us hold on to the hope we say we have and not be changed. We can trust God that He will do what He promised.

HEBREWS 10:23

If we have no faith, He will still be faithful for He cannot go against what He is.

2 TIMOTHY 2:13

The Lord is not slow about keeping His promise as some people think. He is waiting for you. The Lord does not want any person to be punished forever.

He wants all people to be sorry for their sins and turn from them.

2 PETER 3:9

"Thanks be to the Lord. He has given rest to His people Israel. He has done all that He promised. Every word has come true of all His good promise, which He promised through His servant Moses."

1 KINGS 8:56

O Lord, You are my God. I will praise You. I will give thanks to Your name. For You have been faithful to do great things, plans that You made long ago.

ISAIAH 25:1

Those who know Your name will put their trust in You. For You, O Lord, have never left alone those who look for You.

PSALM 9:10

Forever, O Lord, Your Word will never change in heaven. You are faithful to all people for all time. You have made the earth, and it stands.

PSALM 119:89–90

"And the shining-greatness of Israel will not lie or change His mind. For He is not a man that He should change His mind."

1 SAMUEL 15:29

Jesus says yes to all of God's many promises. It is through Jesus that we say, "Let it be so," when we give thanks to God.

2 CORINTHIANS 1:20

"I will not break My agreement, or change what was spoken by My lips."

PSALM 89:34

"The mountains may be taken away and the hills may shake, but My loving-kindness will not be taken from you. And My agreement of peace will not be shaken," says the Lord who has loving-pity on you.

ISAIAH 54:10

"I have spoken, and I will make it happen. I have planned it, and I will do it."

ISAIAH 46:11

FEAR

"Do not be afraid, little flock. Your Father wants to give you the holy nation of God."

LUKE 12:32

"For I am the Lord your God Who holds your right hand, and Who says to you, 'Do not be afraid. I will help you.'"

ISAIAH 41:13

"But he who listens to me will live free from danger, and he will rest easy from the fear of what is sinful."

PROVERBS 1:33

"Do not be afraid of them who kill the body. They are not able to kill the soul."

MATTHEW 10:28

Do not be afraid of fear that comes all at once. And do not be afraid of the storm of the sinful when it comes. For the Lord will be your trust. He will keep your foot from being caught.

PROVERBS 3:25–26

For God did not give us a spirit of fear. He gave us a spirit of power and of love and of a good mind.

2 TIMOTHY 1:7

You will not be afraid when you lie down. When you lie down, your sleep will be sweet.

PROVERBS 3:24

"The Lord watches over those who are right with Him. He hears their prayers. But the Lord is against those who sin." (Psalm 34:12–16) Who will hurt you if you do what is right? But even if you suffer for doing what is right, you will be happy. Do not be afraid or troubled by what they may do to make it hard for you.

1 PETER 3:12–14

"All will be right and good for you. No one over you will make it hard for you, and you will not be afraid. You will be far from trouble, for it will not come near you."

ISAIAH 54:14

You should not act like people who are owned by someone. They are always afraid. Instead, the Holy Spirit makes us His sons, and we can call to Him, "My Father."

ROMANS 8:15

So we can say for sure, "The Lord is my Helper. I am not afraid of anything man can do to me." (Psalm 118:6)

HEBREWS 13:6

God is our safe place and our strength. He is always our help when we are in trouble. So we will not be afraid, even if the earth is shaken and the mountains fall into the center of the sea.

PSALM 46:1–2

"I, even I, am He Who comforts you. Who are you that you are afraid of a man who dies? Why are you afraid of the sons of men who are made like grass?"

ISAIAH 51:12

The fear of man brings a trap, but he who trusts in the Lord will be honored.

PROVERBS 29:25

He will cover you with His wings. And under His wings you will be safe. He is faithful like a safe-covering and a strong wall. You will not be afraid of trouble at night, or of the arrow that flies by day. You will not be afraid of the sickness that walks in darkness, or of the trouble that destroys at noon.

PSALM 91:4–6

"Fear not, for you will not be ashamed. Do not be troubled, for you will not be put to shame."

ISAIAH 54:4

"When you pass through the waters, I will be with you. When you pass through the rivers, they will not flow over you. When you walk through the fire, you will not be burned. The fire will not destroy you."

ISAIAH 43:2

"Peace I leave with you. My peace I give to you. I do not give peace to you as the world gives. Do not let your hearts be troubled or afraid."

JOHN 14:27

Yes, even if I walk through the valley of the shadow of death, I will not be afraid of anything, because You are with me. You have a walking stick with which to guide and one with which to help. These comfort me. You are making a table of food ready for me in front of those who hate me. You have poured oil on my head. I have everything I need.

PSALM 23:4–5

The Lord is my light and the One Who saves me. Whom should I fear? The Lord is the strength of my life. Of whom should I be afraid? Even if an army gathers against me, my heart will not be afraid. Even if war rises against me, I will be sure of You.

PSALM 27:1, 3

But we have power over all these things through Jesus Who loves us so much. For I know that nothing can keep us from the love of God. Death cannot! Life cannot! Angels cannot! Leaders cannot! Any other power cannot! Hard things now or in the future cannot! The world above or the world below cannot! Any other living thing cannot keep us away from the love of God which is ours through Christ Jesus our Lord.

ROMANS 8:37–39

FOOD AND CLOTHING

"You will have much to eat and be filled. And you will praise the name of the Lord your God, Who has done wonderful things for you. Then My people will never be put to shame."

JOEL 2:26

He makes peace within your walls. He fills you with the best grain.

PSALM 147:14

He gives food to those who fear Him. He will remember His agreement forever.

PSALM 111:5

The man who is right with God has all the food he needs, but the stomach of the sinful man never has enough.

PROVERBS 13:25

"I will give her many good things. I will give her poor people much bread."

PSALM 132:15

"Do not worry. Do not keep saying, 'What will we eat?' or, 'What will we drink?' or, 'What will we wear?' The people who do not know God are looking for all these things. Your Father in heaven knows you need all these things."

MATTHEW 6:31—32

FORGIVENESS

"But I tell you, love those who hate you. (*Respect and give thanks for those who say bad things to you. Do good to those who hate you.) Pray for those who do bad things to you and who make it hard for you. Then you may be the sons of your Father Who is in heaven. His sun shines on bad people and on good people. He sends rain on those who are right with God and on those who are not right with God."

MATTHEW 5:44—45

"When you stand to pray, if you have anything against anyone, forgive him. Then your Father in heaven will forgive your sins also."

MARK 11:25

"If you forgive people their sins, your Father in heaven will forgive your sins also."

MATTHEW 6:14

"If the one who hates you is hungry, feed him. If he is thirsty, give him water."

ROMANS 12:20

"But love those who hate you. Do good to them. Let them use your things and do not expect something back. Your reward will be much. You will be the children of the Most High. He is kind to those who are not thankful and to those who are full of sin. You must have loving-kindness just as your Father has loving-kindness. Do not say what is wrong in other people's lives. Then other people will not say what is wrong in your life. Do not say someone is guilty. Then other people will not say you are guilty. Forgive other people and other people will forgive you.

"Give, and it will be given to you. You will have more than enough. It can be pushed down and shaken together and it will still run over as it is given to you. The way you give to others is the way you will receive in return."

LUKE 6:35–38

FRUITFULNESS

"I am the true Vine. My Father is the One Who cares for the Vine. He takes away any branch in Me that does not give fruit. Any branch that gives fruit, He cuts it back so it will give more fruit. You are made clean by the words I have spoken to you. Get your life from Me and I will live in you. No branch can give fruit by itself. It has to get life from the vine. You are able to give fruit only when you have life from Me. I am the Vine and you are the branches. Get your life from Me. Then I will live in you and you will give much fruit. You can do nothing without Me."

JOHN 15:1–5

This man is like a tree planted by rivers of water, which gives its fruit at the right time and its leaf never dries up. Whatever he does will work out well for him.

PSALM 1:3

And they will come and call out for joy on the height of Zion. They will shine with joy over the goodness of the Lord, over the grain, the new wine, and the oil, and over the young of the flock and the cattle. Their life will be like a well-watered garden. They will never have sorrow again.

JEREMIAH 31:12

They will still give fruit when they are old. They will be full of life and strength.

PSALM 92:14

"I will be to Israel like the water on the grass in the early morning. He will grow like the lily, and have roots like the cedars of Lebanon."

HOSEA 14:5

If you have all these things and keep growing in them, they will keep you from being of no use and from having no fruit when it comes to knowing our Lord Jesus Christ.

2 PETER 1:8

GOSSIP

The words of one who speaks about others in secret are like tempting bites of food. They go down into the inside parts of the body.

PROVERBS 18:8

He who goes about talking to hurt people makes secrets known. So do not be with those who talk about others.

PROVERBS 20:19

He who is always telling stories makes secrets known, but he who can be trusted keeps a thing hidden.

PROVERBS 11:13

A bad man spreads trouble. One who hurts people with bad talk separates good friends.

PROVERBS 16:28

Your tongue makes plans to destroy like a sharp knife, you who lie.

PSALM 52:2

The north wind brings rain, and a tongue that hurts people brings angry looks.

PROVERBS 25:23

Keep your tongue from sin and your lips from speaking lies.

PSALM 34:13

When there is no wood, the fire goes out. Where there is no one telling secret stories about people, arguing stops.

PROVERBS 26:20

GRACE, GROWTH IN

"When you give much fruit, My Father is honored. This shows you are My followers."

JOHN 15:8

We must give thanks to God for you always, Christian brothers. It is the right thing to do because your faith is growing so much. Your love for each other is stronger all the time.

2 THESSALONIANS 1:3

Christian brothers, we ask you, because of the Lord Jesus, to keep on living in a way that will please God. I have already told you how to grow in the Christian life.

1 THESSALONIANS 4:1

And I pray that you will be filled with the fruits of right living. These come from Jesus Christ, with honor and thanks to God.

PHILIPPIANS 1:11

Do your best to add holy living to your faith. Then add to this a better understanding.

2 PETER 1:5

"But the one who is right with God will hold to his way. And he who has clean hands will become stronger and stronger."

JOB 17:9

All of us, with no covering on our faces, show the shining-greatness of the Lord as in a mirror. All the time we are being changed to look like Him, with more and more of His shining-greatness. This change is from the Lord Who is the Spirit.

2 CORINTHIANS 3:18

The Lord will finish the work He started for me. O Lord, Your loving-kindness lasts forever. Do not turn away from the works of Your hands.

PSALM 138:8

The Good News came to you the same as it is now going out to all the world. Lives are being changed, just as your life was changed the day you heard the Good News. You understood the truth about God's loving-favor.

COLOSSIANS 1:6

My eyes are on the prize. I want to win the race and get the prize of God's call from heaven through Christ Jesus. All of us who are full-grown Christians should think this way. If you do not think this way, God will show it to you. So let us keep on obeying the same truth we have already been following.

PHILIPPIANS 3:14–16

But the way of those who are right is like the early morning light. It shines brighter and brighter until the perfect day.

PROVERBS 4:18

GUIDANCE

Your ears will hear a word behind you, saying, "This is the way, walk in it," whenever you turn to the right or to the left.

ISAIAH 30:21

This is God, our God forever and ever. He will show us the way until death.

PSALM 48:14

The mind of a man plans his way, but the Lord shows him what to do.

PROVERBS 16:9

The steps of a good man are led by the Lord. And He is happy in his way.

PSALM 37:23

For his God tells him what to do and teaches him the right way.

ISAIAH 28:26

Those right with God, who are without blame, make a straight way for themselves, but the sinful will fall by their own wrong-doing.

PROVERBS 11:5

Agree with Him in all your ways, and He will make your paths straight.

PROVERBS 3:6

I will show you and teach you in the way you should go. I will tell you what to do with My eye upon you.

PSALM 32:8

"I will lead the blind by a way that they do not know. I will lead them in paths they do not know. I will turn darkness into light in front of them. And I will make the bad places smooth. These are the things I will do and I will not leave them."

ISAIAH 42:16

Yet I am always with You. You hold me by my right hand. You will lead me by telling me what I should do. And after this, You will bring me into shining-greatness.

PSALM 73:23−24

GUILT

If we tell Him our sins, He is faithful and we can depend on Him to forgive us of our sins. He will make our lives clean from all sin.

1 JOHN 1:9

Let the sinful turn from his way, and the one who does not know God turn from his thoughts. Let him turn to the Lord, and He will have loving-pity on him. Let him turn to our God, for He will for sure forgive all his sins.

ISAIAH 55:7

"For if you return to the Lord, your brothers and your sons will be shown pity by those who took them away, and will return to this land. For the Lord your God is kind and loving. He will not turn His face away from you if you return to Him."

2 CHRONICLES 30:9

He has taken our sins from us as far as the east is from the west.

PSALM 103:12

Our heart may say that we have done wrong. But remember, God is greater than our heart. He knows everything.

1 JOHN 3:20

"I will show loving-kindness to them and forgive their sins. I will remember their sins no more." (Jeremiah 31:31–34)

HEBREWS 8:12

For if a man belongs to Christ, he is a new person. The old life is gone. New life has begun.

2 CORINTHIANS 5:17

"I will forgive their sins. I will remember their sins no more."

JEREMIAH 31:34

"I will make them clean from all the sins they have done against Me. I will forgive all their sins against Me."

JEREMIAH 33:8

I am writing to you, my children, for your sins have been forgiven because of Christ's name.

1 JOHN 2:12

"I, even I, am the One Who takes away your sins because of Who I am. And I will not remember your sins."

ISAIAH 43:25

If we live in the light as He is in the light, we share what we have in God with each other. And the blood of Jesus Christ, His Son, makes our lives clean from all sin.

1 JOHN 1:7

HELP IN TROUBLES

But the saving of those who are right with God is from the Lord. He is their strength in time of trouble.

PSALM 37:39

The Lord opens the eyes of the blind. The Lord raises up those who are brought down. The Lord loves those who are right and good.

PSALM 146:8

The Lord is good, a safe place in times of trouble. And He knows those who come to Him to be safe.

NAHUM 1:7

When he falls, he will not be thrown down, because the Lord holds his hand.

PSALM 37:24

You are my hiding place. You keep me safe from trouble. All around me are your songs of being made free.

PSALM 32:7

You have shown me many troubles of all kinds. But You will make me strong again. And You will bring me up again from deep in the earth.

PSALM 71:20

Why are you sad, O my soul? Why have you become troubled within me? Hope in God, for I will yet praise Him, my help and my God.

PSALM 42:11

My body and my heart may grow weak, but God is the strength of my heart and all I need forever.

PSALM 73:26

Nothing will hurt you. No trouble will come near your tent. For He will tell His angels to care for you and keep you in all your ways.

PSALM 91:10—11

Love the Lord, all you who belong to Him! The Lord keeps the faithful safe. But He gives the proud their pay in full.

PSALM 31:23

When you lie down among the sheep, you are like the wings of a dove covered with silver, and the end of its wings with shining gold.

PSALM 68:13

"See, God will not turn away from a man who is honest and faithful. And He will not help those who do wrong. He will yet make you laugh and call out with joy."

JOB 8:20–21

For He has not turned away from the suffering of the one in pain or trouble. He has not hidden His face from him. But He has heard his cry for help.

PSALM 22:24

The Lord also keeps safe those who suffer. He is a safe place in times of trouble.

PSALM 9:9

Even if I walk into trouble, You will keep my life safe. You will put out Your hand against the anger of those who hate me. And Your right hand will save me.

PSALM 138:7

You make my lamp bright. The Lord my God lights my darkness.

PSALM 18:28

A man who does what is right and good may have many troubles. But the Lord takes him out of them all.

PSALM 34:19

The Lord is my rock, and my safe place, and the One Who takes me out of trouble. My God is my rock, in Whom I am safe. He is my safe-covering, my saving strength, and my strong tower.

PSALM 18:2

"I have told you these things so you may have peace in Me. In the world you will have much trouble. But take hope! I have power over the world!"

JOHN 16:33

The Lord lifts up those who are suffering, and He brings the sinful down to the ground.

PSALM 147:6

For He Who punishes for the blood of another remembers them. He does not forget the cry of those who suffer.

PSALM 9:12

HOLY SPIRIT

"Listen to my strong words! See, I will pour out my spirit on you. I will make my words known to you."

PROVERBS 1:23

"Then I will ask My Father and He will give you another Helper. He will be with you forever. He is the Spirit of Truth. The world cannot receive Him. It does not see Him or know Him. You know Him because He lives with you and will be in you."

JOHN 14:16–17

"The Holy Writings say that rivers of living water will flow from the heart of the one who puts his trust in Me." Jesus said this about the Holy Spirit Who would come to those who put their trust in Him. The Holy Spirit had not yet been given. Jesus had not yet been raised to the place of honor.

JOHN 7:38–39

"The Holy Spirit is coming. He will lead you into all truth. He will not speak His Own words. He will speak what He hears. He will tell you of things to come."

JOHN 16:13

"And as for Me, this is My agreement with them," says the Lord. "My Spirit which is upon you, and My words which I have put in your mouth, will not leave your mouth, or the mouth of your children, or the mouth of your children's children," says the Lord, "from now and forever."

ISAIAH 59:21

"You are sinful and you know how to give good things to your children. How much more will your Father in heaven give the Holy Spirit to those who ask Him?"

LUKE 11:13

"Whoever drinks the water that I will give him will never be thirsty. The water that I will give him will become in him a well of life that lasts forever."

JOHN 4:14

"And I will put My Spirit within you and cause you to follow My Laws and be careful to do what I tell you."

EZEKIEL 36:27

Because of the price Christ Jesus paid, the good things that came to Abraham might come to the people who are not Jews. And by putting our trust in Christ, we receive the Holy Spirit He has promised.

GALATIANS 3:14

Christ gave you the Holy Spirit and He lives in you. You do not need anyone to teach you. The Holy Spirit is able to teach you all things. What He teaches you is truth and not a lie. Live by the help of Christ as the Holy Spirit has taught you.

1 JOHN 2:27

For the holy nation of God is not food and drink. It is being right with God. It is peace and joy given by the Holy Spirit.

ROMANS 14:17

In the same way, the Holy Spirit helps us where we are weak. We do not know how to pray or what we should pray for, but the Holy Spirit prays to God for us with sounds that cannot be put into words. God knows the hearts of men. He knows what the Holy Spirit is thinking. The Holy Spirit prays for those who belong to Christ the way God wants Him to pray.

ROMANS 8:26—27

We have not received the spirit of the world. God has given us His Holy Spirit that we may know about the things given to us by Him.

1 CORINTHIANS 2:12

You should not act like people who are owned by someone. They are always afraid. Instead, the Holy Spirit makes us His sons, and we can call to Him, "My Father."

ROMANS 8:15

HONESTY

"Do not steal. Be honest in what you do. Do not lie to one another."

LEVITICUS 19:11

"O sinful house, can I forget the riches you got by wrong-doing? You lied about the weight of things, which I hate. Can I make a man not guilty who lies and has false weights in his bag? The rich men of the city have hurt many people. Her people are liars. Their tongues in their mouths speak false words."

MICAH 6:10−12

"Do not lie about the weight or price of anything."

LEVITICUS 19:35

The Lord hates a false weight, but a true weight is His joy.

PROVERBS 11:1

"You must have a full and fair weight. You must have a fair way to show how big something is. Then you will live long in the land the Lord your God gives you. For the Lord hates everyone who does such things, who lies and is not fair."

DEUTERONOMY 25:15–16

The sinful ask for something, but do not return it. But those who are right with God are kind and give.

PSALM 37:21

No man should do wrong to his Christian brother in anything. The Lord will punish a person who does. I have told you this before. For God has not called us to live in sin. He has called us to live a holy life.

1 THESSALONIANS 4:6–7

Do not lie to each other. You have put out of your life your old ways. You have now become a new person and are always learning more about Christ. You are being made more like Christ. He is the One Who made you.

COLOSSIANS 3:9–10

Do not keep good from those who should have it,
when it is in your power to do it.

PROVERBS 3:27

"If you sell anything to your neighbor, or buy from
your neighbor, do not do wrong to one another."

LEVITICUS 25:14

"Do not do wrong to one another, but fear your
God. I am the Lord your God."

LEVITICUS 25:17

He who walks with God, and whose words are good
and honest, he who will not take money received
from wrong-doing, and will not receive money
given in secret for wrong-doing, he who stops his
ears from hearing about killing, and shuts his eyes
from looking at what is sinful, he will have a place
on high. His safe place will be a rock that cannot
be taken over. He will be given food and will have
water for sure.

ISAIAH 33:15–16

A little earned in a right way is better than much
earned in a wrong way.

PROVERBS 16:8

HOPE

Why are you sad, O my soul? Why have you become troubled within me? Hope in God, for I will yet praise Him, my help and my God.

PSALM 42:11

Because of Christ, you have put your trust in God. He raised Christ from the dead and gave Him great honor. So now your faith and hope are in God.

1 PETER 1:21

Get your minds ready for good use. Keep awake. Set your hope now and forever on the loving-favor to be given you when Jesus Christ comes again.

1 PETER 1:13

The sinful is thrown down by his wrong-doing, but the man who is right with God has a safe place when he dies.

PROVERBS 14:32

We thank God for the hope that is being kept for you in heaven. You first heard about this hope through the Good News which is the Word of Truth.

COLOSSIANS 1:5

Christ in you brings hope of all the great things to come.

COLOSSIANS 1:27

Be strong in heart, all you who hope in the Lord.

PSALM 31:24

For You are my hope, O Lord God. You are my trust since I was young.

PSALM 71:5

Let us thank the God and Father of our Lord Jesus Christ. It was through His loving-kindness that we were born again to a new life and have a hope that never dies. This hope is ours because Jesus was raised from the dead.

1 PETER 1:3

HOSPITALITY

Be happy to have people stay for the night and eat with you. God has given each of you a gift. Use it to help each other. This will show God's loving-favor.

I PETER 4:9–10

What if a Christian does not have clothes or food?
And one of you says to him, "Goodbye, keep yourself warm and eat well." But if you do not give him
what he needs, how does that help him?

JAMES 2:15–16

"For sure, I tell you, whoever gives you a cup of
water to drink in My name because you belong to
Christ will not lose his pay from God."

MARK 9:41

"In every way I showed you that by working hard
like this we can help those who are weak. We must
remember what the Lord Jesus said, 'We are more
happy when we give than when we receive.'"

ACTS 20:35

What if a person has enough money to live on and
sees his brother in need of food and clothing? If he
does not help him, how can the love of God be in
him?

I JOHN 3:17

This does not mean that others do not have to give
and you have to give much. You should share alike.
You have more than you need now. When you have

need, then they can help you. You should share alike.

2 CORINTHIANS 8:13–14

Share what you have with Christian brothers who are in need. Give meals and a place to stay to those who need it.

ROMANS 12:13

"For I was hungry and you gave Me food to eat. I was thirsty and you gave Me water to drink. I was a stranger and you gave Me a room. I had no clothes and you gave Me clothes to wear. I was sick and you cared for Me. I was in prison and you came to see Me."

MATTHEW 25:35–36

"Then the King will say, 'For sure, I tell you, because you did it to one of the least of My brothers, you have done it to Me.' "

MATTHEW 25:40

Do not forget to be kind to strangers and let them stay in your home. Some people have had angels in their homes without knowing it.

HEBREWS 13:2

HUMILITY

"Whoever is without pride as this little child is the greatest in the holy nation of heaven."

MATTHEW 18:4

O Lord, You have heard the prayers of those who have no pride. You will give strength to their heart, and You will listen to them.

PSALM 10:17

"The person who thinks he is important will find out how little he is worth. The person who is not trying to honor himself will be made important."

MATTHEW 23:12

"For God puts down the man who is filled with pride. But He saves the one who is not proud."

JOB 22:29

But He gives us more loving-favor. For the Holy Writings say, "God works against the proud but gives loving-favor to those who have no pride."

JAMES 4:6

The reward for not having pride and having the fear of the Lord is riches, honor and life.

PROVERBS 22:4

The fear of the Lord is the teaching for wisdom, and having no pride comes before honor.

PROVERBS 15:33

A man's pride will bring him down, but he whose spirit is without pride will receive honor.

PROVERBS 29:23

So put away all pride from yourselves. You are standing under the powerful hand of God. At the right time He will lift you up.

1 PETER 5:6

"Those who have no pride in their hearts are happy, because the earth will be given to them."

MATTHEW 5:5

For the Lord is happy with His people. He saves those who have no pride and makes them beautiful.

PSALM 149:4

He leads those without pride into what is right, and teaches them His way.

PSALM 25:9

Look for the Lord, all you people of the earth who are not proud, and who have obeyed His Laws. Look for what is right and good. Have no pride. You may be kept safe on the day of the Lord's anger.

ZEPHANIAH 2:3

But those who have no pride will be given the earth. And they will be happy and have much more than they need.

PSALM 37:11

JEALOUSY

"Do not have a desire for your neighbor's wife. Do not desire your neighbor's house, his field, his man servant, his bull, his donkey, or anything that belongs to your neighbor."

DEUTERONOMY 5:21

Wherever you find jealously and fighting, there will be trouble and every other kind of wrong-doing.

JAMES 3:16

Do you think the Holy Writings mean nothing when they said, "The Holy Spirit Whom God has given to live in us has a strong desire for us to be faithful to Him"?

JAMES 4:5

Rest in the Lord and be willing to wait for Him. Do not trouble yourself when all goes well with the one who carries out his sinful plans.

PSALM 37:7

The sinful man is proud of the desires of his heart. He praises those who want everything but he speaks against the Lord.

PSALM 10:3

Do not be jealous of a man who hurts others, and do not choose any of his ways.

PROVERBS 3:31

A heart that has peace is life to the body, but wrong desires are like the wasting away of the bones.

PROVERBS 14:30

I have seen that all the work done is because a man wants what his neighbor has. This also is for nothing, like trying to catch the wind.

ECCLESIASTES 4:4

Anger causes trouble and a bad temper is like a flood, but who can stand when there is jealousy?

PROVERBS 27:4

Let us not become proud in ways in which we should not. We must not make hard feelings among ourselves as Christians or make anyone jealous.

GALATIANS 5:26

Do not be jealous of sinful men. Do not want to be with them.

PROVERBS 24:1

If you have jealously in your heart and fight to have many things, do not be proud of it. Do not lie against the truth.

JAMES 3:14

Do not let your heart be jealous of sinners, but live in the fear of the Lord always. For sure there is a future and your hope will not be cut off.

PROVERBS 23:17–18

Jesus said to His followers, "Because of this, I say to you, do not worry about your life, what you are going to eat. Do not worry about your body, what you are going to wear. Life is worth more than food. The body is worth more than clothes."

LUKE 12:22–23

JOY

"You will go out with joy, and be led out in peace. The mountains and the hills will break out into sounds of joy before you. And all the trees of the field will clap their hands."

ISAIAH 55:12

How happy are the people who know the sound of joy! They walk in the light of Your face, O Lord. They are full of joy in Your name all day long. And by being right with You, they are honored.

PSALM 89:15–16

The joy of being saved is being heard in the tents of those who are right and good. The right hand of the Lord does powerful things.

PSALM 118:15

You have filled my heart with more happiness than they have when there is much grain and wine.

PSALM 4:7

Those who plant with tears will gather fruit with songs of joy. He who goes out crying as he carries his bag of seed will return with songs of joy as he brings much grain with him.

PSALM 126:5–6

Light is spread like seed for those who are right and good, and joy for the pure in heart. Be glad in the Lord, you who are right and good. Give thanks to His holy name.

PSALM 97:11–12

"Then you will have joy in the All-powerful, and lift up your face to God."

JOB 22:26

"I have told you these things so My joy may be in you and your joy may be full."

JOHN 15:11

Yet I will have joy in the Lord. I will be glad in the God Who saves me.

HABAKKUK 3:18

So the people, for whom the Lord paid the price to be saved, will return. They will come with songs of joy to Zion. Joy that lasts forever will be on their heads. They will receive joy and happiness, and sorrow and sad voices will hurry away.

ISAIAH 51:11

For our heart is full of joy in Him, because we trust in His holy name.

PSALM 33:21

You have never seen Him but you love Him. You cannot see Him now but you are putting your trust in Him. And you have joy so great that words cannot tell about it.

1 PETER 1:8

"Do not be sad for the joy of the Lord is your strength."

NEHEMIAH 8:10

I will have much joy in the Lord. My soul will have joy in my God, for He has clothed me with the clothes of His saving power. He has put around me a coat of what is right and good, as a man at his own wedding wears something special on his head, and as a bride makes herself beautiful with stones of great worth.

ISAIAH 61:10

The man who is right and good will be glad in the Lord and go to Him to be safe. All those whose hearts are right will give Him praise.

PSALM 64:10

But let those who are right and good be glad. Let them be happy before God. Yes, let them be full of joy.

PSALM 68:3

"You are sad now. I will see you again and then your hearts will be full of joy. No one can take your joy from you."

JOHN 16:22

LAZINESS

Do your best to live a quiet life. Learn to do your own work well. We told you about this before. By doing this, you will be respected by those who are not Christians. Then you will not be in need and others will not have to help you.

1 THESSALONIANS 4:11–12

Do not be lazy but always work hard. Work for the Lord with a heart full of love for Him.

ROMANS 12:11

The soul of the lazy person has strong desires but gets nothing, but the soul of the one who does his best gets more than he needs.

PROVERBS 13:4

He who works with a lazy hand is poor, but the hand of the hard worker brings riches. A son who gathers in summer is wise, but a son who sleeps during gathering time brings shame.

PROVERBS 10:4-5

When we were with you, we told you that if a man does not work, he should not eat. We hear that some are not working. But they are spending their time trying to see what others are doing. Our words to such people are that they should be quiet and go to work. They should eat their own food. In the name of the Lord Jesus Christ we say this.

2 THESSALONIANS 3:10-12

He who works his land will have more than enough food, but he who wastes his time will become very poor.

PROVERBS 28:19

A hard-working farmer should receive first some of what he gathers from the field.

2 TIMOTHY 2:6

I passed by the field of the lazy man, by the grape-vines of the man without understanding. And see, it was all grown over with thorns. The ground was covered with weeds, and its stone wall was broken down. When I saw it, I thought about it. I looked and received teaching. "A little sleep, a little rest, a little folding of the hands to rest," and your being poor will come as a robber, and your need like a man ready to fight.

PROVERBS 24:30—34

Do not love sleep, or you will become poor. Open your eyes, and you will be filled with food.

PROVERBS 20:13

The path of the lazy man is grown over with thorns, but the path of the faithful is a good road.

PROVERBS 15:19

The hand of those who do their best will rule, but the lazy hand will be made to work.

PROVERBS 12:24

He who works his land will have all the bread he needs, but he who follows what is of no worth has no wisdom.

PROVERBS 12:11

This is what I have seen to be good and right: to eat and to drink and be happy in all the work one does under the sun during the few years of his life which God has given him. For this is his pay. As for every man to whom God has given riches and many good things, He has also given him the power to eat from them, receive his pay and be happy in his work. This is the gift of God.

ECCLESIASTES 5:18–19

LONELINESS

"I will not leave you without help as children without parents. I will come to you."

JOHN 14:18

"Then you will call, and the Lord will answer. You will cry, and He will say, 'Here I am.'"

ISAIAH 58:9

"You are of great worth in My eyes. You are honored and I love you."

ISAIAH 43:4

"I will be a Father to you. You will be My sons and daughters, says the All-powerful God."

2 CORINTHIANS 6:18

"See, I am with you. I will care for you everywhere you go. And I will bring you again to this land. For

I will not leave you until I have done all the things I promised you."

GENESIS 28:15

When you have Christ, you are complete. He is the head over all leaders and powers.

COLOSSIANS 2:10

Because I suffer and am in need, let the Lord think of me. You are my help and the One Who sets me free. O my God, do not wait.

PSALM 40:17

LONG LIFE

"Even when you are old I will be the same. And even when your hair turns white, I will help you. I will take care of what I have made. I will carry you, and will save you."

ISAIAH 46:4

"Wisdom is with old men, and understanding with long life. With God are wisdom and strength. Wise words and understanding belong to Him."

JOB 12:12–13

The honor of young men is their strength. And the honor of old men is their hair turning white.

PROVERBS 20:29

Grandchildren are the pride and joy of old men and a son is proud of his father.

PROVERBS 17:6

"Walk in all the way the Lord your God has told you. Then you may live, it may be well with you, and you may live a long time in the land that will belong to you."

DEUTERONOMY 5:33

O God, You have taught me from when I was young. And I still tell about Your great works. Even when I am old and my hair is turning white, O God, do not leave me alone. Let me tell about Your strength to all the people living now, and about Your power to all who are to come.

PSALM 71:17–18

My son, do not forget my teaching. Let your heart keep my words. For they will add to you many days and years of life and peace.

PROVERBS 3:1–2

"Then you and your son and your grandson will fear the Lord your God. You will obey all His Laws that I tell you, all the days of your life. And then you will have a longer life."

DEUTERONOMY 6:2

I will please him with a long life. And I will show him My saving power.

PSALM 91:16

The fear of the Lord makes life longer, but the years of the sinful will be cut off.

PROVERBS 10:27

For by me your days will grow in number, and years will be added to your life.

PROVERBS 9:11

LOVE, BROTHERLY

"I give you a new Law. You are to love each other. You must love each other as I have loved you. If you love each other, all men will know you are My followers."

JOHN 13:34–35

Be sure your love is true love. Hate what is sinful. Hold on to whatever is good. Love each other as Christian brothers. Show respect for each other.

ROMANS 12:9–10

You do not need anyone to write to you about loving your Christian brothers. God has taught you to love each other.

1 THESSALONIANS 4:9

But whoever loves his brother is in the light. And there will be no reason to sin because of him.

1 JOHN 2:10

You have made your souls pure by obeying the truth through the Holy Spirit. This has given you a true love for the Christians. Let it be a true love from the heart.

1 PETER 1:22

Dear friends, let us love each other, because love comes from God. Those who love are God's children and they know God. Those who do not love do not know God because God is love.

1 JOHN 4:7–8

My children, let us not love with words or in talk only. Let us love by what we do and in truth.

1 JOHN 3:18

Dear friends, if God loved us that much, then we should love each other.

1 JOHN 4:11

God has chosen you. You are holy and loved by Him. Because of this, your new life should be full of loving-pity. You should be kind to others and have no pride. Be gentle and be willing to wait for others. Try to understand other people. Forgive each other. If you have something against someone, forgive him. That is the way the Lord forgave you.

COLOSSIANS 3:12–13

LOVE, GOD'S

"For God so loved the world that He gave His only Son. Whoever puts his trust in God's Son will not be lost but will have life that lasts forever."

JOHN 3:16

"He will love you and bring good to you and make you a nation of many. He will bring good to your children and the fruit of your land, your grain, your

new wine and your oil. And He will give you many
cattle and young ones in your flock, in the land He
promised to your fathers to give you."

DEUTERONOMY 7:13

The Lord opens the eyes of the blind. The Lord raises
up those who are brought down. The Lord loves
those who are right and good.

PSALM 146:8

For as a young man marries a young woman who
has never had a man, your sons will marry you. And
as the man to be married finds joy in his bride, so
your God will find joy in you.

ISAIAH 62:5

The Lord came to us from far away, saying, "I have
loved you with a love that lasts forever. So I have
helped you come to Me with loving-kindness."

JEREMIAH 31:3

Our Lord Jesus Christ and God our Father loves us.
Through His loving favor He gives us comfort and
hope that lasts forever. May He give your hearts comfort and strength to say and do every good thing.

2 THESSALONIANS 2:16–17

The Lord your God is with you, a Powerful One
Who wins the battle. He will have much joy over

you. With His love He will give you new life. He will have joy over you with loud singing.

ZEPHANIAH 3:17

"I will bring My people back to Me. I will not hold back My love from them, for I am no longer angry with them."

HOSEA 14:4

The Lord hates the way of the sinful, but He loves him who follows what is right and good.

PROVERBS 15:9

"I will have joy in doing good to them. And I will be faithful to plant them in this land with all My heart and with all My soul."

JEREMIAH 32:41

But God had so much loving-kindness. He loved us with such a great love. Even when we were dead because of our sins, He made us alive by what Christ did for us. You have been saved from the punishment of sin by His loving-favor. God raised us up from death when He raised up Christ Jesus. He has given us a place with Christ in the heavens. He did this to show us through all the time to come the great riches of His loving-favor. He has shown us His kindness through Christ Jesus.

EPHESIANS 2:4–7

This is love! It is not that we loved God but that He loved us. For God sent His Son to pay for our sins with His own blood.

1 JOHN 4:10

"The Father loves you. He loves you because you love Me and believe that I came from the Father."

JOHN 16:27

We have come to know and believe the love God has for us. God is love. If you live in love, you live by the help of God and God lives in you.

1 JOHN 4:16

We love Him because He loved us first.

1 JOHN 4:19

"I have made Your name known to them and will make it known. So then the love You have for Me may be in them and I may be in them."

JOHN 17:26

"I am in them and You are in Me so they may be one and be made perfect. Then the world may know that You sent Me and that You love them as You love Me."

JOHN 17:23

LOVING GOD

"Know then that the Lord your God is God, the faithful God. He keeps His promise and shows His loving-kindness to those who love Him and keep His Laws, even to a thousand family groups in the future."

DEUTERONOMY 7:9

"I love those who love me, and those who look for me with much desire will find me."

PROVERBS 8:17

"The one who loves Me is the one who has My teaching and obeys it. My Father will love whoever loves Me. I will love him and will show Myself to him."

JOHN 14:21

"I give riches to those who love me, and fill their store-houses."

PROVERBS 8:21

Be happy in the Lord. And He will give you the desires of your heart.

PSALM 37:4

The Lord takes care of all who love Him. But He will destroy all the sinful.

PSALM 145:20

May God give loving-favor to all who love our Lord Jesus Christ with a love that never gets weak.

EPHESIANS 6:24

Because he has loved Me, I will bring him out of trouble. I will set him in a safe place on high, because he has known My name.

PSALM 91:14

The Holy Writings say, "No eye has ever seen or no ear has ever heard or no mind has ever thought of the wonderful things God has made ready for those who love Him."

1 CORINTHIANS 2:9

"Listen to and obey all the Laws I am telling you today. Love the Lord your God. Work for Him with all your heart and soul. If you do, He will give the rain for your land at the right times, the early and late rain. So you may gather in your grain, your new wine and your oil. He will give grass in your fields for your cattle. And you will eat and be filled."

DEUTERONOMY 11:13–15

LUST

For everything that is in the world does not come from the Father. The desires of our flesh and the things our eyes see and want and the pride of this life come from the world. The world and all its desires will pass away. But the man who obeys God and does what He wants done will live forever.

1 JOHN 2:16–17

"You have heard that it was said long ago, 'You must not do sex sins.' But I tell you, anyone who even looks at a woman with a sinful desire of wanting her has already sinned in his heart."

MATTHEW 5:27–28

Do not desire her beauty in your heart. Do not let her catch you with her eyes. For because of a woman who sells the use of her body, one is brought down to a loaf of bread. A sinful woman hunts to take a man's very life. Can a man carry fire in his arms, and his clothes not be burned? Can a man walk on hot coals, and his feet not be burned? So is he who goes in to his neighbor's wife. Whoever touches her will be punished.

PROVERBS 6:25-29

Through His shining-greatness and perfect life, He has given us promises. These promises are of great worth and no amount of money can buy them. Through these promises you can have God's own life in you now that you have gotten away from the sinful things of the world which came from wrong desires of the flesh.

2 PETER 1:4

So give yourselves to God. Stand against the devil and he will run away from you. Come close to God and He will come close to you. Wash your hands, you sinners. Clean up your hearts, you who want to follow the sinful ways of the world and God at the same time.

JAMES 4:7-8

Turn away from the sinful things young people want to do. Go after what is right. Have a desire for faith and love and peace. Do this with those who pray to God from a clean heart.

2 TIMOTHY 2:22

There was a time when we were foolish and did not obey. We were fooled in many ways. Strong desires held us in their power. We wanted only to please ourselves. We wanted what others had and were angry when we could not have them. We hated others and they hated us. But God, the One Who saves, showed how kind He was and how He loved us by saving us from the punishment of sin. It was not because we worked to be right with God. It was because of His loving-kindness that He washed our sins away. At the same time He gave us new life when the Holy Spirit came into our lives.

TITUS 3:3–5

At one time all of us lived to please our old selves. We gave in to what our bodies and minds wanted. We were sinful from birth like all other people and would suffer from the anger of God. But God had so much loving-kindness. He loved us with such a great love. Even when we were dead because of our sins, He made us alive by what Christ did for us. You have been saved from the punishment of sin by His loving-favor. God raised us up from death when He raised up Christ Jesus. He has given us a place with Christ in the heavens.

EPHESIANS 2:3–6

God's free gift of being saved is being given to everyone. We are taught to have nothing to do with that which is against God. We are to have nothing to do with the desires of this world. We are to be wise and to be right with God. We are to live God-like lives in this world.

TITUS 2:11–12

Those of us who belong to Christ have nailed our sinful old selves on His cross. Our sinful desires are now dead.

GALATIANS 5:24

I say this to you: Let the Holy Spirit lead you in each step. Then you will not please your sinful old selves. The things our old selves want to do are against what the Holy Spirit wants. The Holy Spirit does not agree with what our sinful old selves want. These two are against each other. So you cannot do what you want to do.

GALATIANS 5:16–17

Dear friends, your real home is not here on earth. You are strangers here. I ask you to keep away from all the sinful desires of the flesh. These things fight to get hold of your soul.

1 PETER 2:11

LYING

Do not lie to each other. You have put out of your life your old ways. You have now become a new person and are always learning more about Christ. You are being made more like Christ. He is the One Who made you.

COLOSSIANS 3:9–10

"Do not lie when you make a promise in My name, and so put the name of your God to shame. I am the Lord."

LEVITICUS 19:12

A man who tells a lie against his neighbor is like a heavy stick or a sword or a sharp arrow.

PROVERBS 25:18

" 'Do not make sinful plans against one another in your hearts. And do not love to make false promises. For I hate all these things,' says the Lord."

ZECHARIAH 8:17

A faithful man who tells what he knows will not lie, but the man who is not faithful will lie.

PROVERBS 14:5

Then the king said to him, "How many times must I tell you to speak nothing but the truth in the name of the Lord?"

1 KINGS 22:16

A man who tells lies about someone will be punished. He who tells lies will not get away.

PROVERBS 19:5

"Do not tell a lie about someone else. Do not join with the sinful to say something that will hurt someone."

EXODUS 23:1

"If an angry person speaks against a man, saying that he did something wrong, then both men who are arguing should stand before the Lord, in front of the religious leaders and the judges who are at work at that time. The judges will choose careful questions to ask about the problem. If the man lied who said his brother is guilty, then you should do to him just what he wanted to do to his brother. In this way you will get rid of the sin among you."

DEUTERONOMY 19:16–19

"But those who are afraid and those who do not have faith and the sinful-minded people and those who kill other people and those who do sex sins and those who follow witchcraft and those who worship false gods and all those who tell lies will be put into the lake of fire and sulphur. This is the second death."

REVELATION 21:8

A man who tells lies about someone will be punished. He who tells lies will be lost.

PROVERBS 19:9

Do not speak against your neighbor without a reason, and do not lie with your lips.

PROVERBS 24:28

The sinful go wrong as soon as they are born. Those who speak lies go the wrong way from birth.

PSALM 58:3

If you have jealousy in your heart and fight to have many things, do not be proud of it. Do not lie against the truth.

JAMES 3:14

Lips that tell the truth will last forever, but a lying tongue lasts only for a little while.

PROVERBS 12:19

MARRIAGE

Enjoy life with the woman you love all the days of your life that will soon be over. God has given you these days under the sun. This is the good you will get in life and in your work which you have done under the sun.

ECCLESIASTES 9:9

Drink water from your own pool, flowing water from your own well.

PROVERBS 5:15

Let your well be honored, and be happy with the wife you married when you were young. Let her be like a loving, female deer. Let her breasts please you at all times. Be filled with great joy always because of her love. My son, why should you be carried away with a sinful woman and fall into the arms of a strange woman?

PROVERBS 5:18−20

The husband should please his wife as a husband. The wife should please her husband as a wife.

1 CORINTHIANS 7:3

Wives, obey your own husbands. In doing this, you obey the Lord. For a husband is the head of his wife as Christ is the head of the church. It is His body (the church) that He saves.

EPHESIANS 5:22—23

Husbands, love your wives. You must love them as Christ loved the church. He gave His life for it.

EPHESIANS 5:25

So men should love their wives as they love their own bodies. He who loves his wife loves himself.

EPHESIANS 5:28

For this reason, a man must leave his father and mother when he gets married and be joined to his wife. The two become one.

EPHESIANS 5:31

Anyone who does not take care of his family and those in his house has turned away from the faith. He is worse than a person who has never put his trust in Christ.

1 TIMOTHY 5:8

Wives, obey your husbands. This is what the Lord wants you to do. Husbands, love your wives. Do not hold hard feelings against them.

COLOSSIANS 3:18—19

In the same way, husbands should understand and respect their wives, because women are weaker than men. Remember, both husband and wife are to share together the gift of life that lasts forever. If this is not done, you will find it hard to pray.

1 Peter 3:7

Older women are to teach the young women to love their husbands and children. They are to teach them to think before they act, to be pure, to be workers at home, to be kind, and to obey their own husbands. In this way, the Word of God is honored.

Titus 2:4–5

MERCY

So the Lord wants to show you kindness. He waits on high to have loving-pity on you. For the Lord is a God of what is right and fair. And good will come to all those who hope in Him.

Isaiah 30:18

"If only God would speak...He would show you the secrets of wisdom because there are two sides. Then

you would know that God is punishing you less than
you should get."

JOB 11:5–6

The Lord has loving-pity on those who fear Him, as
a father has loving-pity on his children.

PSALM 103:13

But the loving-kindness of the Lord is forever and forever on those who fear Him. And what is right with
God is given forever to their children's children.

PSALM 103:17

And God said, "I will have My goodness pass in front of
you. I will make the name of the Lord known in front
of you. I will have loving-kindness and loving-pity for
anyone I want to."

EXODUS 33:19

"I will plant her for Myself in the land. Those who
were not loved, I will call, 'My loved ones.' Those
who were not My people, I will call, 'My people.'
And they will say, 'You are my God!' "

HOSEA 2:23

"People from strange lands will build up your walls,
and their kings will help you. For I destroyed you
in My anger, but in My favor I have had loving-pity
on you."

ISAIAH 60:10

"Because of My name I hold back My anger. For My praise I keep Myself from cutting you off."

ISAIAH 48:9

MONEY

Do not work hard to be rich. Stop trying to get things for yourself. When you set your eyes upon it, it is gone. For sure, riches make themselves wings like an eagle that flies toward the heavens.

PROVERBS 23:4–5

The few things that the man right with God has is better than the riches of many sinful men.

PSALM 37:16

Listen, my dear Christian brothers, God has chosen those who are poor in the things of this world to be rich in faith. The holy nation of heaven is theirs. That is what God promised to those who love Him.

JAMES 2:5

He who laughs at the poor brings shame to his Maker. He who is glad at trouble will be punished.

PROVERBS 17:5

Do not rob the poor because he is poor, or crush those who suffer at the gate.

PROVERBS 22:22

Tell those who are rich in this world not to be proud and not to trust in their money. Money cannot be trusted. They should put their trust in God. He gives us all we need for our happiness. Tell them to do good and be rich in good works. They should give much to those in need and be ready to share. Then they will be gathering together riches for themselves. These good things are what they will build on for the future. Then they will have the only true life!

1 TIMOTHY 6:17–19

The sleep of the working man is pleasing, if he eats little or much. But the full stomach of the rich man does not let him sleep. There is something very wrong which I have seen under the sun: Riches being kept by the owner and he is hurt by them. When those riches are lost because he used them in a wrong way, and he had become the father of a son, there was nothing left for him.

ECCLESIASTES 5:12–14

"But remember the Lord your God. For it is He Who is giving you power to become rich. By this

He may keep His agreement which He promised to your fathers, as it is this day."

DEUTERONOMY 8:18

But those in need will not always be forgotten. The hope of the poor will not be lost forever.

PSALM 9:18

"But He saves from the sword those in need. He saves the poor from the power of the strong. So those who have no hope, have hope, and what is not right and good must shut its mouth."

JOB 5:15–16

He who trusts in his riches will fall, but those who are right with God will grow like a green leaf.

PROVERBS 11:28

A faithful man will have many good things, but he who hurries to be rich will be punished for it.

PROVERBS 28:20

He who loves money will never have enough money to make him happy. It is the same for the one who loves to get many things. This also is for nothing.

ECCLESIASTES 5:10

He who makes it hard for the poor by getting more for himself, or who gives to the rich, will become poor himself.

PROVERBS 22:16

A man with a sinful eye hurries to be rich. He does not know that he will be in need.

PROVERBS 28:22

The rich and the poor meet together. The Lord is the maker of them all.

PROVERBS 22:2

A little with the fear of the Lord is better than great riches with trouble.

PROVERBS 15:16

A poor man who walks in his honor is better than a rich man who is sinful in his ways.

PROVERBS 28:6

Happy is the man who cares for the poor. The Lord will save him in times of trouble.

PSALM 41:1

Your beauty should come from the inside. It should come from the heart. This is the kind that lasts. Your beauty should be a gentle and quiet spirit. In God's sight this is of great worth and no amount of money can buy it.

1 PETER 3:4

Obedience

"See, I have put in front of you today life and what is good, and death and what is bad. I tell you today to love the Lord your God. Walk in His ways. Keep all His Laws and all that He has decided. Then you will live and become many. And the Lord your God will bring good to you in the land you are going in to take."

DEUTERONOMY 30:15–16

"Do what is right and good in the eyes of the Lord. Then it will be well with you. And you may go in and take the good land for your own which the Lord promised to give to your fathers."

DEUTERONOMY 6:18

"If you listen to these Laws and keep and obey them, the Lord your God will keep His agreement and loving-kindness as He promised to your fathers."

DEUTERONOMY 7:12

"If only they had such a heart in them that they would fear Me and live by all My Laws always! Then it would go well with them and with their children forever."

DEUTERONOMY 5:29

"So be careful to keep the words of this agreement and obey them so all that you do will go well."

DEUTERONOMY 29:9

Keep on doing all the things you learned and received and heard from me. Do the things you saw me do. Then the God Who gives peace will be with you.

PHILIPPIANS 4:9

"Anyone who breaks even the least of the Law of Moses and teaches people not to do what it says, will be called the least in the holy nation of heaven. He who obeys and teaches others to obey what the Law of Moses says, will be called great in the holy nation of heaven."

MATTHEW 5:19

"If they hear and serve Him, the rest of their days will be filled with what they need and their years with peace."

JOB 36:11

"If you obey My teaching, you will live in My love. In this way, I have obeyed my Father's teaching and live in His love."

JOHN 15:10

"If you know these things, you will be happy if you do them."

JOHN 13:17

But the one who keeps looking into God's perfect Law and does not forget it will do what it says and be happy as he does it. God's Word makes men free.

JAMES 1:25

We will receive from Him whatever we ask if we obey Him and do what He wants.

1 JOHN 3:22

Just to hear the Law does not make a man right with God. The man right with God is the one who obeys the Law.

ROMANS 2:13

"For sure, I tell you, anyone who hears My Word and puts his trust in Him Who sent Me has life that lasts forever. He will not be guilty. He has already passed from death into life."

JOHN 5:24

"Whoever does what My father in heaven wants him to do is My brother and My sister and My mother."

MATTHEW 12:50

The world and all its desires will pass away. But the man who obeys God and does what He wants done will live forever.

1 John 2:17

"Not everyone who says to me, 'Lord, Lord,' will go into the holy nation of heaven. The one who does the things My Father in heaven wants him to do will go into the holy nation of heaven."

Matthew 7:21

And having been made perfect, He planned and made it possible for all those who obey Him to be saved from the punishment of sin.

Hebrews 5:9

PARENTS' DUTIES

"For I have chosen him, so that he may teach his children and the sons of his house after him to keep the way of the Lord by doing what is right and fair."

Genesis 18:19

We will not hide them from their children. But we will tell the children-to-come the praises of the Lord, and of His power and the great things He has done. For He has made His will known to Jacob. He made the Law in Israel, which He told our fathers to teach their children. So the children-to-come might know, even the children yet to be born. So they may rise up and tell it to their children. Then they would put their trust in God and not forget the works of God. And they would keep His Law.

PSALM 78:4–7

"Teach them to your children. Talk about them when you sit in your house and when you walk on the road and when you lie down and when you get up."

DEUTERONOMY 11:19

Bring up a child by teaching him the way he should go, and when he is old he will not turn away from it.

PROVERBS 22:6

"Only be careful. Keep watch over your life. Or you might forget the things you have seen. Do not let them leave your heart for the rest of your life. But teach them to your children and to your grandchildren. Remember the day you stood before the Lord your God at Mount Sinai. The Lord said to me, 'Gather the people together before Me, so I may let them hear My words. Then they may learn to fear Me all the days they live on the earth, and they may teach their children.' "

DEUTERONOMY 4:9–10

Punish your son when he does wrong and he will give you comfort. Yes, he will give joy to your soul.

PROVERBS 29:17

Fathers, do not be too hard on your children so they will become angry. Teach them in their growing years with Christian teaching.

EPHESIANS 6:4

Fathers, do not be so hard on your children that they will give up trying to do what is right.

COLOSSIANS 3:21

PATIENCE

Christian brothers, be willing to wait for the Lord to come again. Learn from the farmer. He waits for the good fruit of the earth until the early and late rains come. You must be willing to wait also. Be strong in your hearts because the Lord is coming again soon.

JAMES 5:7–8

Do not let yourselves get tired of doing good. If we do not give up, we will get what is coming to us at the right time.

GALATIANS 6:9

Let us hold on to the hope we say we have and not be changed. We can trust God that He will do what He promised.

HEBREWS 10:23

"But the one who stays true to the end will be saved."

MATTHEW 24:13

You must be willing to wait without giving up. After you have done what God wants you to do, God will give you what He promised you.

HEBREWS 10:36

My Christian brothers, you should be happy when you have all kinds of tests. You know these prove your faith. It helps you not to give up. Learn well how to wait so you will be strong and complete and in need of nothing.

JAMES 1:2–4

We are glad for our troubles also. We know that troubles help us learn not to give up. When we have learned not to give up, it shows we have stood the test. When we have stood the test, it gives us hope.

ROMANS 5:3–4

PEACE

"I will make the lips to praise. Peace, peace to him who is far and to him who is near," says the Lord, "and I will heal him."

ISAIAH 57:19

Let the peace of Christ have power over your hearts. You were chosen as a part of His body. Always be thankful.

COLOSSIANS 3:15

The peace of God is much greater than the human mind can understand. This peace will keep your hearts and minds through Christ Jesus.

PHILIPPIANS 4:7

The work of being right and good will give peace. From the right and good work will come quiet trust forever.

ISAIAH 32:17

Look at the man without blame. And watch the man who is right and good. For the man of peace will have much family to follow him.

PSALM 37:37

May the Lord of peace give you His peace at all times. The Lord be with you all.

2 THESSALONIANS 3:16

"Peace I leave with you. My peace I give to you. I do not give peace to you as the world gives. Do not let your hearts be troubled or afraid."

JOHN 14:27

I will listen to what God the Lord will say. For He will speak peace to His people, to those who are right with Him.

PSALM 85:8

POVERTY

For He will take out of trouble the one in need when he cries for help, and the poor man who has no one to help. He will have loving-pity on the weak and those in need. He will save the lives of those in need.

PSALM 72:12–13

But He lifts those in need out of their troubles. He makes their families grow like flocks.

PSALM 107:41

For the Lord hears those who are in need, and does not hate His people in prison.

PSALM 69:33

Sing to the Lord! Praise the Lord! For He has taken the soul of the one in need from the hand of the sinful.

JEREMIAH 20:13

He will answer the prayer of those in need. He will not turn from their prayer.

PSALM 102:17

He raises the poor from the dust. He lifts those in need from the ashes.

PSALM 113:7

"I will give her many good things. I will give her poor people much bread."

PSALM 132:15

O God, You gave the poor what they needed because You are good.

PSALM 68:10

But He will judge the poor in a right and good way. He will be fair in what He decides for the people of the earth who have much trouble.

ISAIAH 11:4

Those who suffer will eat and have enough. Those who look for the Lord will praise Him. May your heart live forever!

PSALM 22:26

Those who have suffered will be happier in the Lord. Those who are in need will have joy in the Holy One of Israel.

ISAIAH 29:19

PRAYER

"Ask, and what you are asking for will be given to you. Look, and what you are looking for you will find. Knock, and the door you are knocking on will be opened to you. Everyone who asks receives what he asks for. Everyone who looks finds what he is looking for. Everyone who knocks has the door opened to him."

MATTHEW 7:7–8

"All things you ask for in prayer, you will receive if you have faith."

MATTHEW 21:22

We are sure that if we ask anything that He wants us to have, He will hear us. If we are sure He hears us when we ask, we can be sure He will give us what we ask for.

1 JOHN 5:14–15

"Then you will call upon Me and come and pray to Me, and I will listen to you."

JEREMIAH 29:12

"And it will be before they call, I will answer. While they are still speaking, I will hear."

ISAIAH 65:24

"You will pray to Him, and He will hear you. And you will keep your promises to Him."

JOB 22:27

"If you get your life from Me and My Words live in you, ask whatever you want. It will be done for you."

JOHN 15:7

Tell your sins to each other. And pray for each other so you may be healed. The prayer from the heart of a man right with God has much power.

JAMES 5:16

"Whatever you ask in My name, I will do it so the shining greatness of the Father may be seen in the Son."

JOHN 14:13

"When you pray, go into a room by yourself. After you have shut the door, pray to your Father Who is in secret. Then your Father Who sees in secret will reward you."

MATTHEW 6:6

"Call on Me in the day of trouble. I will take you out of trouble, and you will honor Me."

PSALM 50:15

"Then you will call, and the Lord will answer. You will cry, and He will say, 'Here I am.' "

ISAIAH 58:9

The Lord is far from the sinful, but He hears the prayer of those who are right with Him.

PROVERBS 15:29

He will call upon Me, and I will answer him.

PSALM 91:15

O You Who hears prayer, to You all men come.

PSALM 65:2

"You are bad and you know how to give good things to your children. How much more will your Father in heaven give good things to those who ask Him?"

MATTHEW 7:11

Those who are right with the Lord cry, and He hears them. And He takes them from all their troubles.

PSALM 34:17

The Lord is near to all who call on Him, to all who call on Him in truth. He will fill the desire of those who fear Him. He will also hear their cry and will save them.

PSALM 145:18–19

"Your Father knows what you need before you ask Him."

MATTHEW 6:8

We will receive from Him whatever we ask if we obey Him and do what He wants.

1 JOHN 3:22

"Call to Me, and I will answer you. And I will show you great and wonderful things which you do not know."

JEREMIAH 33:3

"Because of this, I say to you, whatever you ask for

when you pray, have faith that you will receive it. Then you will get it."

MARK 11:24

PRIDE

Pride comes before being destroyed and a proud spirit comes before a fall.

PROVERBS 16:18

It is bad for those who are wise in their own eyes, and who think they know a lot!

ISAIAH 5:21

Do you see a man who is wise in his own eyes? There is more hope for a fool than for him.

PROVERBS 26:12

"Look on everyone who is proud, and bring him down. Crush the sinful where they stand."

JOB 40:12

"Proud," "Self-important" and "One who laughs at the truth" are the names of the man who acts without respect and is proud.

PROVERBS 21:24

You speak sharp words to the proud, the hated ones, because they turn from Your Word.

PSALM 119:21

A proud man starts fights, but all will go well for the man who trusts in the Lord. He who trusts in his own heart is a fool, but he who walks in wisdom will be kept safe.

PROVERBS 28:25—26

"The fear of the Lord is to hate what is sinful. I hate pride, self-love, the way of sin, and lies."

PROVERBS 8:13

Let another man praise you, and not your own mouth. Let a stranger, and not your own lips.

PROVERBS 27:2

Jesus said to them, "You are the kind of people who make yourselves look good before other people. God knows your hearts. What men think is good is hated in the eyes of God."

LUKE 16:15

If anyone wants to be proud, he should be proud of what the Lord has done. It is not what a man thinks and says of himself that is important. It is what God thinks of him.

2 CORINTHIANS 10:17—18

"How can you believe when you are always wanting honor from each other? And yet you do not look for the honor that comes from the only God."

JOHN 5:44

Jesus sat down and called the followers to Him. He said, "If anyone wants to be first, he must be last of all. He will be the one to care for all."

MARK 9:35

PRISONERS

The Lord says, "Even those taken away by the strong man will be taken from him. Those taken by the powerful ruler will be saved. For I will fight with the one who fights with you, and I will save your sons."

ISAIAH 49:25

"Even if you are driven to the ends of the earth, the Lord your God will gather you and bring you back."

DEUTERONOMY 30:4

For the Lord hears those who are in need, and does not hate His people in prison.

PSALM 69:33

He brought them out of darkness and the shadow of death. And He broke their chains.

PSALM 107:14

He helps those who have a bad power over them. He gives food to the hungry. And He sets those in prison free.

PSALM 146:7

God makes a home for those who are alone. He leads men out of prison into happiness and well-being. But those who fight against Him live in an empty desert.

PSALM 68:6

PROTECTION, GOD'S

The name of the Lord is a strong tower. The man who does what is right runs into it and is safe.

PROVERBS 18:10

"You will laugh at danger and times of no food. And you will not be afraid of wild animals."

JOB 5:22

"Then you would trust, because there is hope. You would look around and rest and be safe. You would lie down and no one would make you afraid. Many would ask for your favor."

JOB 11:18–19

The Lord will keep you from all that is sinful. He will watch over your soul. The Lord will watch over your coming and going, now and forever.

PSALM 121:7–8

You will not be afraid when you lie down. When you lie down, your sleep will be sweet.

PROVERBS 3:24

Who will hurt you if you do what is right?

1 PETER 3:13

"May the one the Lord loves live by Him and be safe. The Lord covers him all the day long. And he lives between His shoulders."

DEUTERONOMY 33:12

He will not be afraid of bad news. His heart is strong because he trusts in the Lord.

PSALM 112:7

Because you have made the Lord your safe place, and the Most High the place where you live, nothing will hurt you. No trouble will come near your tent.

PSALM 91:9–10

But now the Lord Who made you, O Jacob, and He Who made you, O Israel, says, "Do not be afraid. For I have bought you and made you free. I have called you by name. You are Mine! When you pass through the waters, I will be with you. When you pass through the rivers, they will not flow over you. When you walk through the fire, you will not be burned. The fire will not destroy you."

ISAIAH 43:1–2

"They will no longer be under the power of the nations. And the wild animals of the earth will not eat them. But they will be safe, and no one will make them afraid."

EZEKIEL 34:28

"But he who listens to me will live free from danger, and he will rest easy from the fear of what is sinful."

PROVERBS 1:33

I will lie down and sleep in peace. O Lord, You alone keep me safe.

PSALM 4:8

Teach me your way, O Lord. Lead me in a straight path, because of those who fight against me.

PSALM 27:11

REPENTANCE

He said, "The time has come. The holy nation of God is near. Be sorry for your sins, turn from them, and believe the Good News."

MARK 1:15

They preached that men should be sorry for their sins and turn from them.

MARK 6:12

The Lord is near to those who have a broken heart. And He saves those who are broken in spirit.

PSALM 34:18

He heals those who have a broken heart. He heals their sorrows.

PSALM 147:3

"And if you put away the sin that is in your hand, do not let wrong-doing be in your tents. Then you will be able to lift up your face without sin. You would be strong and not afraid."

JOB 11:14–15

"But if the sinful man turns from all the sins he has done and obeys all My Laws and does what is right and good, he will live for sure. He will not die. None of the sins he has done will be remembered against him. Because of the right and good things he has done, he will live."

EZEKIEL 18:21–22

RIGHTEOUSNESS

For the Lord God is a sun and a safe-covering. The Lord gives favor and honor. He holds back nothing good from those who walk in the way that is right.

PSALM 84:11

The young lions suffer want and hunger. But they who look for the Lord will not be without any good thing.

PSALM 34:10

What the sinful man is afraid of will come upon him, and what is wanted by the man who is right with God will be given to him.

PROVERBS 10:24

Trouble follows sinners, but good things will be given to those who are right with God.

PROVERBS 13:21

A good man will get favor from the Lord, but He will punish a man who makes sinful plans.

PROVERBS 12:2

"First of all, look for the holy nation of God. Be right with Him. All these other things will be given to you also."

MATTHEW 6:33

He who trusts in his riches will fall, but those who are right with God will grow like a green leaf.

PROVERBS 11:28

And men will say, "For sure there is pay for those who are right and good. For sure there is a God Who says who is guilty or not on the earth."

PSALM 58:11

For You will make those happy who do what is right, O Lord. You will cover them all around with Your favor.

PSALM 5:12

Paul and Apollos and Peter belong to you. The world and life and death belong to you. Things now and things to come belong to you. You belong to Christ, and Christ belongs to God.

1 CORINTHIANS 3:22–23

God did not keep His own Son for Himself but gave Him for us all. Then with His Son, will He not give us all things?

ROMANS 8:32

Tell those who are right and good that it will go well for them. For they will enjoy the fruit of what they do.

ISAIAH 3:10

For sure, You will give me goodness and loving-kindness all the days of my life. Then I will live with You in Your house forever.

PSALM 23:6

Jesus said to him, "For sure, I tell you, unless a man is born again, he cannot see the holy nation of God." Nicodemus said to Him, "How can a man be born when he is old? How can he get into his mother's body and be born the second time?" Jesus answered, "For sure, I tell you, unless a man is born of water and of the Spirit of God, he cannot get into the holy nation of God. Whatever is born of the flesh is flesh. Whatever is born of the Spirit is spirit. Do not be surprised that I said to you, 'You must be born again.' "

JOHN 3:3–7

For if a man belongs to Christ, he is a new person. The old life is gone. New life has begun.

2 CORINTHIANS 5:17

It is good when you pray like this. It pleases God Who is the One Who saves. He wants all people to be saved from the punishment of sin. He wants them to come to know the truth.

1 TIMOTHY 2:3–4

My dear children, I am writing this to you so you will not sin. But if anyone does sin, there is One Who will go between him and the Father. He is Jesus Christ, the One Who is right with God. He paid for our sins with His own blood. He did not pay for ours only, but for the sins of the whole world.

1 JOHN 2:1–2

Christ never sinned but God put our sin on Him. Then we are made right with God because of what Christ has done for us.

2 CORINTHIANS 5:21

When you were dead in your sins, you were not set free from the sinful things of the world. But God forgave your sins and gave you new life through Christ.

COLOSSIANS 2:13

These words are true and they can be trusted. Because of this, we work hard and do our best because our hope is in the living God, the One Who would save all men. He saves those who believe in Him.

1 TIMOTHY 4:9–10

God's free gift is not like the sin of Adam. Many people died because of the sin of this one man, Adam. But the loving-favor of God came to many people also. This gift came also by one Man Jesus Christ, God's Son.

ROMANS 5:15

But God, the One Who saves, showed how kind He was and how He loved us by saving us from the punishment of sin. It was not because we worked to be right with God. It was because of His loving-kindness that He washed our sins away. At the same time He gave us new life when the Holy Spirit came into our lives. God gave the Holy Spirit to fill our lives through Jesus Christ, the One Who saves.

TITUS 3:4–6

SEEKING GOD

"The Lord is with you when you are with Him. If you look for Him, He will let you find Him. But if you leave Him, He will leave you."

2 CHRONICLES 15:2

A man cannot please God unless he has faith. Anyone who comes to God must believe that He is. That one must also know that God gives what is promised to the one who keeps on looking for Him.

HEBREWS 11:6

"They were to look for God. Then they might feel after Him and find Him because He is not far from each one of us."

ACTS 17:27

The Lord says to the people of Israel, "Look for Me and live."

AMOS 5:4

"But from there you will look for the Lord your God. And you will find Him if you look for Him with all your heart and soul."

DEUTERONOMY 4:29

"The hand of our God brings good to all who look for Him. But His power and His anger are against all who turn away from Him."

EZRA 8:22

"As for you, my son Solomon, know the God of your father. Serve Him with a whole heart and a willing mind. For the Lord looks into all hearts, and understands every plan and thought. If you look to Him, He will let you find Him. But if you turn away from Him, He will turn away from you forever."

1 CHRONICLES 28:9

"If you will look for God and pray to the All-powerful, if you are pure and right and good, for sure He will help you. Because you are right and good He will put you back where you should be."

JOB 8:5–6

Those who know Your name will put their trust in You. For You, O Lord, have never left alone those who look for You.

PSALM 9:10

The Lord is good to those who wait for Him, to the one who looks for Him.

LAMENTATIONS 3:25

SELF-DENIAL

Jesus said to His followers, "If anyone wants to be My follower, he must forget about himself. He must take up his cross and follow Me. If anyone wants to keep his life safe, he will lose it. If anyone gives up his life because of Me, he will save it. For what does a man have if he gets all the world and loses his own soul? What can a man give to buy back his soul?"

MATTHEW 16:24–26

So then, Christian brothers, we are not to do what our sinful old selves want us to do. If you do what your sinful old selves want you to do, you will die in sin. But if, through the power of the Holy Spirit, you destroy those actions to which the body can be led, you will have life.

ROMANS 8:12–13

Those of us who belong to Christ have nailed our sinful old selves on His cross. Our sinful desires are now dead.

GALATIANS 5:24

God's free gift of being saved is being given to everyone. We are taught to have nothing to do with that which is against God. We are to have nothing to do with the desires of this world. We are to be wise and to be right with God. We are to live God-like lives in this world.

TITUS 2:11–12

Jesus said to them, "For sure, I tell you, anyone who has left his house or parents or brothers or wife or children because of the holy nation of God will receive much more now. In the time to come he will have life that lasts forever."

LUKE 18:29–30

"But I tell you, do not fight with the man who wants to fight. Whoever hits you on the right side of the face, turn so he can hit the other side also. If any person takes you to court to get your shirt, give him your coat also. Whoever makes you walk a short way, go with him twice as far."

MATTHEW 5:39–41

SELF-RIGHTEOUSNESS

"For sure you have spoken in my hearing. I have heard all you have said. You said, 'I am pure and without sin. I am not guilty, and there is no sin in me.' "

JOB 33:8–9

"Do you think this is right? Do you say, 'I am more right than God'?"

JOB 35:2

It is bad for those who are wise in their own eyes, and who think they know a lot!

ISAIAH 5:21

"For sure God will not listen to an empty cry. The All-powerful will not do anything about it."

JOB 35:13

Do you see a man who is wise in his own eyes? There is more hope for a fool than for him.

PROVERBS 26:12

If anyone thinks he is important when he is nothing, he is fooling himself.

GALATIANS 6:3

If anyone wants to be proud, he should be proud of what the Lord has done. It is not what a man thinks and says of himself that is important. It is what God thinks of him.

2 CORINTHIANS 10:17—18

All of us have become like one who is unclean. All our right and good works are like dirty pieces of cloth. And all of us dry up like a leaf. Our sins take us away like the wind.

ISAIAH 64:6

A proud man starts fights, but all will go well for the man who trusts in the Lord. He who trusts in his own heart is a fool, but he who walks in wisdom will be kept safe.

PROVERBS 28:25—26

Jesus said to them, "You are the kind of people who make yourselves look good before other people. God knows your hearts. What men think is good is hated in the eyes of God."

LUKE 16:15

Let another man praise you, and not your own mouth. Let a stranger, and not your own lips.

PROVERBS 27:2

Jesus said to them, "If you were blind, you would not be guilty of sin. But because you say, 'We see,' you still are guilty of your sin."

JOHN 9:41

SEXUAL SINS

The body was not meant for sex sins. It was meant to work for the Lord. The Lord is for our body.

1 CORINTHIANS 6:13

Have nothing to do with sex sins! Any other sin that a man does, does not hurt his own body. But the man who does a sex sin sins against his own body. Do you not know that your body is a house of God where the Holy Spirit lives? God gave you His Holy Spirit. Now you belong to God. You do not belong to yourselves. God bought you with a great price. So honor God with your body. You belong to Him.

1 CORINTHIANS 6:18−20

This is what I say to those who are not married and to women whose husbands have died. It is good if you do not get married. I am not married. But if you are not able to keep from doing that which you know is wrong, get married. It is better to get married than to have such strong sex desires.

1 CORINTHIANS 7:8−9

God wants you to be holy. You must keep away from sex sins.

1 THESSALONIANS 4:3

It is good if a man does not get married. But because of being tempted to sex sins, each man should get married and have his own wife. Each women should get married and have her own husband.

1 CORINTHIANS 7:1−2

But if a man has the power to keep from getting married and knows in his mind that he should not, he is wise if he does not get married.

1 CORINTHIANS 7:37

You have never been tempted to sin in any different way than other people. God is faithful. He will not allow you to be tempted more than you can take. But when you are tempted, He will make a way for you to keep from falling into sin.

1 CORINTHIANS 10:13

These are men who have kept themselves pure by not being married. They follow the Lamb wherever He goes. They have been bought by the blood of Christ and have been made free from among men. They are the first ones to be given to God and to the Lamb.

REVELATION 14:4

Marriage should be respected by everyone. God will punish those who do sex sins and are not faithful in marriage.

HEBREWS 13:4

Do you not know that your bodies are a part of Christ Himself? Am I to take a part of Christ and make it a part of a woman who sells the use of her body? No! Never!

1 CORINTHIANS 6:15

SHAME

The Holy Writings say, "No one who puts his trust in Christ will ever be put to shame." (Isaiah 28:16)

ROMANS 10:11

Then I will not be put to shame when I respect Your Word.

PSALM 119:6

Hope never makes us ashamed because the love of God has come into our hearts through the Holy Spirit Who was given to us.

ROMANS 5:5

For this reason, I am suffering. But I am not ashamed. I know the One in Whom I have put my trust. I am sure He is able to keep safe that which I have trusted to Him until the day He comes again.

2 TIMOTHY 1:12

The person who puts his trust in the Rock (Christ) will not be put to shame." (Isaiah 28:16)

ROMANS 9:33

Do your best to know that God is pleased with you. Be as a workman who has nothing to be ashamed of. Teach the words of truth in the right way.

2 TIMOTHY 2:15

But if a man suffers as a Christian, he should not be ashamed. He should thank God that he is a Christian.

1 PETER 4:16

Let my heart be without blame in Your Law. Do not let me be put to shame.

PSALM 119:80

SICKNESS

Is anyone among you sick? He should send for the church leaders and they should pray for him. They should pour oil on him in the name of the Lord. The prayer given in faith will heal the sick man, and the Lord will raise him up. If he has sinned, he will be forgiven. Tell your sins to each other. And pray for each other so you may be healed. The prayer from the heart of a man right with God has much power.

JAMES 5:14–16

Heal me, O Lord, and I will be healed. Save me and I will be saved. For You are my praise.

JEREMIAH 17:14

"But this is to show you that the Son of Man has power on earth to forgive sins." He said to the sick man, "Get up! Take your bed and go home." He got up and went to his home.

MATTHEW 9:6–7

"Serve the Lord your God and He will give you bread and water. And I will take sickness from among you."

EXODUS 23:25

Jesus went over all Galilee. He taught in their places of worship and preached the Good News of the holy nation. He healed all kinds of sickness and disease among the people. The news about Him went over all the country of Syria. They brought all the sick people to Him with many kinds of diseases and pains. They brought to Him those who had demons. They brought those who at times lose the use of their minds. They brought those who could not use their hands and legs. He healed them.

MATTHEW 4:23–24

"For I will heal you. I will heal you where you have been hurt," says the Lord.

JEREMIAH 30:17

SIN, FREEDOM FROM

"Then I will put clean water on you, and you will be clean. I will make you clean from all your unclean ways and from all your false gods. I will give you a new heart and put a new spirit within you. I will take away your heart of stone and give you a heart of flesh."

EZEKIEL 36:25–26

"All the early preachers spoke of this. Everyone who puts his trust in Christ will have his sins forgiven through His name."

ACTS 10:43

We know that our old life, our old sinful self, was nailed to the cross with Christ. And so the power of sin that held us was destroyed. Sin is no longer our boss. When a man is dead, he is free from the power of sin.

ROMANS 6:6–7

For if a man belongs to Christ, he is a new person. The old life is gone. New life has begun.

2 CORINTHIANS 5:17

What does this mean? Are we to keep on sinning so that God will give us more of His loving favor? No, not at all! We are dead to sin. How then can we keep on living in sin?

ROMANS 6:1—2

You must do the same thing! Think of yourselves as dead to the power of sin. But now you have new life because of Jesus Christ our Lord. You are living this new life for God.

ROMANS 6:11

Sin must not have power over you. You are not living by the Law. You have life because of God's loving-favor.

ROMANS 6:14

SIN, REDEMPTION FROM

"A Son will be born to her. You will give Him the name Jesus because He will save His people from the punishment of their sins."

MATTHEW 1:21

"Men and brothers, listen to this. You may be forgiven

of your sins by this One I am telling you about."

ACTS 13:38

You know that Christ came to take away our sins. There is no sin in Him.

1 JOHN 3:5

My dear children, I am writing this to you so you will not sin. But if anyone does sin, there is One Who will go between him and the Father. He is Jesus Christ, the One Who is right with God.

1 JOHN 2:1–2

He carried our sins in His own body when He died on a cross. In doing this, we may be dead to sin and alive to all that is right and good. His wounds have healed you!

1 PETER 2:24

What I say is true and all the world should receive it. Christ Jesus came into the world to save sinners from their sin and I am the worst sinner.

1 TIMOTHY 1:15

The next day John the Baptist saw Jesus coming to him. He said, "See! The Lamb of God Who takes away the sin of the world!"

JOHN 1:29

But He was hurt for our wrong-doing. He was crushed for our sins. He was punished so we would have peace. He was beaten so we would be healed. All of us like sheep have gone the wrong way. Each of us has turned to his own way. And the Lord has put on Him the sin of us all.

ISAIAH 53:5–6

Because of the blood of Christ, we are bought and made free from the punishment of sin. And because of His blood, our sins are forgiven. His loving-favor to us is so rich.

EPHESIANS 1:7

He gave Himself to die for our sins. He did this so we could be saved from this sinful world.

GALATIANS 1:4

It is the same with Christ. He gave Himself once to take away the sins of many. When He comes the second time, He will not need to give Himself again for sin. He will save all those who are waiting for Him.

HEBREWS 9:28

And by one gift He has made perfect forever all those who are being set apart for God-like living.

HEBREWS 10:14

SLANDER AND REPROACH

"You are happy when people act and talk in a bad way to you and make it very hard for you and tell bad things and lies about you because you trust in Me. Be glad and full of joy because your reward will be much in heaven. They made it very hard for the early preachers who lived a long time before you."

MATTHEW 5:11–12

But even if you suffer for doing what is right, you will be happy. Do not be afraid or troubled by what they may do to make it hard for you.

1 PETER 3:14

He will send from heaven and save me. He will put to shame him who is breaking me under his feet. God will send His loving-kindness and His truth.

PSALM 57:3

"Listen to Me, you who know what is right and good, you people who have My Law in your hearts. Do not fear the shame of strong words from man. Do not be troubled when they speak against you."

ISAIAH 51:7

You will hide them with You in secret from the sinful plans of men. You keep them in Your tent in secret from those who fight with tongues.

PSALM 31:20

"You will be hidden from the punishment of the tongue. You will not be afraid of being destroyed when danger comes."

JOB 5:21

He will make your being right and good show as the light, and your wise actions as the noon day.

PSALM 37:6

SUCCESS

Great riches are in the house of those who are right with God, but trouble is what the sinful will receive.

PROVERBS 15:6

The pay for not having pride and having the fear of the Lord is riches, honor and life.

PROVERBS 22:4

Then He will give you rain for the seed you will plant in the ground. And He will give you bread from the grain from the ground. It will be good, and more than you need. In that day your cattle will eat in a large field.

Isaiah 30:23

And I know that every man who eats and drinks sees good in all his work. It is the gift of God.

Ecclesiastes 3:13

"The Lord will give much to you. He will give you many children, and many young ones among your animals, and much food from the ground, in the land the Lord promised to your fathers to give you. The Lord will open for you His good store-house, the heavens. He will give rain to your land at the right time. He will bring good to all the work you do. You will give to many nations. But you will not use anything that belongs to them. The Lord will make you the head and not the tail. If you listen to the Laws of the Lord your God which I tell you today and be careful to obey them, you will only be above and not below."

Deuteronomy 28:11–13

"And the Lord your God will bring much good upon all the work you do, and upon your children, and the young of your cattle, and the food of your field.

For the Lord will again be happy to bring good to you, just as He was happy with your fathers."

DEUTERONOMY 30:9

As for every man to whom God has given riches and many good things, He has also given him the power to eat from them, receive his pay and be happy in his work. This is the gift of God.

ECCLESIASTES 5:19

"You will decide something, and it will be done for you. Light will shine on your path."

JOB 22:28

"Riches and honor are mine, lasting riches and being right with God. My fruit is better than gold, even pure gold. What I give is better than fine silver."

PROVERBS 8:18–19

Riches and well-being are in his house. And his right-standing with God will last forever.

PSALM 112:3

"Put your gold in the dust, and gold of Ophir among the stones of the river. Then the All-powerful will be your gold and silver of much worth."

JOB 22:24–25

"He will give grass in your fields for your cattle. And you will eat and be filled."

DEUTERONOMY 11:15

For you will eat the fruit of your hands. You will be happy and it will be well with you.

PSALM 128:2

"They will build houses and live in them. They will plant grapes and eat their fruit. They will not build a house and another live in it. They will not plant and another eat. For My people will live a long time, like the days of a tree. And for a long time My chosen ones will enjoy the work of their hands. They will not work for nothing, or give birth to children and have trouble. For they will be the children of those who receive good from the Lord, and their children with them."

ISAIAH 65:21–23

"All these good things will come upon you if you will obey the Lord your God. Good will come to you in the city, and good will come to you in the country. Good will come to your children, and the fruit of your ground, and the young of your animals. Your cattle and flock will have many young ones. Good will come to your basket and your bread pan. Good will come to you when you come in, and when you go out."

DEUTERONOMY 28:2–6

TRUST

For the Lord God is a sun and a safe-covering. The Lord gives favor and honor. He holds back nothing good from those who walk in the way that is right. O Lord of all, how happy is the man who trusts in You!

PSALM 84:11–12

Trust in the Lord, and do good. So you will live in the land and will be fed. Be happy in the Lord. And He will give you the desires of your heart. Give your way over to the Lord. Trust in Him also. And He will do it.

PSALM 37:3–5

Trust in the Lord with all your heart, and do not trust in your own understanding. Agree with Him in all your ways, and He will make your paths straight.

PROVERBS 3:5–6

How happy is the man who has made the Lord his trust, and has not turned to the proud or to the followers of lies.

PSALM 40:4

Those who trust in the Lord are like Mount Zion, which cannot be moved but stands forever.

PSALM 125:1

The work of being right and good will give peace. From the right and good work will come quiet trust forever.

ISAIAH 32:17

You are now children of God because you have put your trust in Christ Jesus.

GALATIANS 3:26

But as for you, hold on to what you have learned and know to be true. Remember where you learned them. You have known the Holy Writings since you were a child. They are able to give you wisdom that leads to being saved from the punishment of sin by putting your trust in Christ Jesus.

2 TIMOTHY 3:14–15

"For God so loved the world that He gave His only Son. Whoever puts his trust in God's Son will not be lost but will have life that lasts forever."

JOHN 3:16

"All the early preachers spoke of this. Everyone who puts his trust in Christ will have his sins forgiven through His name."

ACTS 10:43

The Holy Writings say, "See! I put in Jerusalem a Stone that people will trip over. It is a Rock that will make them fall. But the person who puts his trust in the Rock (Christ) will not be put to shame." (Isaiah 28:16)

ROMANS 9:33

He gave the right and the power to become children of God to those who received Him. He gave this to those who put their trust in His name.

JOHN 1:12

"Whoever puts his trust in His Son is not guilty. Whoever does not put his trust in Him is guilty already. It is because he does not put his trust in the name of the only Son of God."

JOHN 3:18

"He who puts his trust in the Son has life that lasts forever. He who does not put his trust in the Son will not have life, but the anger of God is on him."

JOHN 3:36

The Holy Writings say, "See, I lay down in Jerusalem a Stone of great worth, worth far more than any amount of money. Anyone who puts his trust in Him will not be ashamed." (Isaiah 28:16)

1 PETER 2:6

"Put your trust in the Lord Jesus Christ and you and your family will be saved from the punishment of sin."

ACTS 16:31

"I came to the world to be a Light. Anyone who puts his trust in Me will not be in darkness."

JOHN 12:46

Jesus said to them, "I am the Bread of Life. He who comes to Me will never be hungry. He who puts his trust in Me will never be thirsty."

JOHN 6:35

"For sure, I tell you, he who puts his trust in Me has life that lasts forever."

JOHN 6:47

WISDOM

If you do not have wisdom, ask God for it. He is always ready to give it to you and will never say you are wrong for asking.

JAMES 1:5

"He will teach us about His ways, that we may walk in His paths. For the Law will go out from Zion, and the Word of the Lord from Jerusalem."

ISAIAH 2:3

I will show you and teach you in the way you should go. I will tell you what to do with My eye upon you.

PSALM 32:8

For God has given wisdom and much learning and joy to the person who is good in God's eyes.

ECCLESIASTES 2:26

Then you will understand the fear of the Lord, and find what is known of God. For the Lord gives wisdom. Much learning and understanding come from His mouth. He stores up perfect wisdom for those who are right with Him. He is a safe-covering to those who are right in their walk.

PROVERBS 2:5–7

See, You want truth deep within the heart. And You will make me know wisdom in the hidden part.

PSALM 51:6

We know God's Son has come. He has given us the understanding to know Him Who is the true God. We are joined together with the true God through His

Son, Jesus Christ. He is the true God and the life that lasts forever.

1 JOHN 5:20

I will give honor and thanks to the Lord, Who has told me what to do. Yes, even at night my mind teaches me.

PSALM 16:7

It was God Who said, "The light will shine in darkness." (Genesis 1:3) He is the One Who made His light shine in our hearts. This brings us the light of knowing God's shining-greatness which is seen in Christ's face.

2 CORINTHIANS 4:6

Sinful men do not understand what is right and fair, but those who look to the Lord understand all things.

PROVERBS 28:5

WORD OF GOD

I am not ashamed of the Good News. It is the power of God. It is the way He saves men from the punishment of their sins if they put their trust in Him. It is for the Jew first and for all other people also.

ROMANS 1:16

The man who reads this Book and listens to it being read and obeys what it says will be happy. For all these things will happen soon.

REVELATION 1:3

All this helps us know that what the early preachers said was true. You will do well to listen to what they have said. Their words are as lights that shine in a dark place. Listen until you understand what they have said. Then it will be like the morning light which takes away the darkness. And the Morning Star (Christ) will rise to shine in your hearts.

2 PETER 1:19

God's Word is living and powerful. It is sharper than a sword that cuts both ways. It cuts straight into where the soul and spirit meet and it divides them. It cuts into the joints and bones. It tells what the heart is thinking about and what it wants to do.

HEBREWS 4:12

The opening up of Your Word gives light. It gives understanding to the child-like.

PSALM 119:130

For the word is a lamp. The teaching is a light, and strong words that punish are the way of life.

PROVERBS 6:23

Your Word is a lamp to my feet and a light to my path.

PSALM 119:105

"You do read the Holy Writings. You think you have life that lasts forever just because you read them. They do tell of Me."

JOHN 5:39

So then, faith comes to us by hearing the Good News. And the Good News comes by someone preaching it.

ROMANS 10:17

As new babies want milk, you should want to drink the pure milk which is God's Word so you will grow up and be saved from the punishment of sin.

1 PETER 2:2

"Keep these words of mine in your heart and in your soul. Tie them as something special to see upon your hand and on your forehead between your eyes."

DEUTERONOMY 11:18

"This book of the Law must not leave your mouth. Think about it day and night, so you may be careful to do all that is written in it. Then all will go well with you. You will receive many good things."

JOSHUA 1:8

Put out of your life all that is unclean and wrong. Receive with a gentle spirit the Word that was taught. It has the power to save your souls from the punishment of sin. Obey the Word of God. If you hear only and do not act, you are only fooling yourself. Anyone who hears the Word of God and does not obey is like a man looking at his face in a mirror. After he sees himself and goes away, he forgets what he looks like. But the one who keeps looking into God's perfect Law and does not forget it will do what it says and be happy as he does it. God's Word makes men free.

JAMES 1:21–25

You have known the Holy Writings since you were a child. They are able to give you wisdom that leads to being saved from the punishment of sin by putting your trust in Christ Jesus. All the Holy Writings are God-given and are made alive by Him. Man is helped when he is taught God's Word. It shows what is wrong. It changes the way of a man's life. It shows him how to be right with God.

2 TIMOTHY 3:15–16

You have been given a new birth. It was from a seed that cannot die. This new life is from the Word of God which lives forever.

1 PETER 1:23

"And now, my brothers, I give you over to God and to the word of His love. It is able to make you strong and to give you what you are to have, along with all those who are set apart for God."

ACTS 20:32

WORK

Then God honored the seventh day and made it holy, because in it He rested from all His work which He had done.

GENESIS 2:3

"The Lord will open for you His good store-house, the heavens. He will give rain to your land at the right time. He will bring good to all the work you do. You will give to many nations. But you will not use anything that belongs to them."

DEUTERONOMY 28:12

"But you be strong. Do not lose strength of heart. For you will be paid for your work."

2 Chronicles 15:7

All the work he began in the house of God, obeying the Laws and looking to his God, he did with all his heart and all went well for him.

2 Chronicles 31:21

Jesus said, "My food is to do what God wants Me to do and to finish His work."

John 4:34

Then the people said to Him, "What are the works God wants us to do?" Jesus said to them, "This is the work of God, that you put your trust in the One He has sent."

John 6:28–29

"I honored You on earth. I did the work You gave Me to do. Now, Father, honor Me with the honor I had with You before the world was made."

John 17:4–5

A young man makes himself known by his actions and proves if his ways are pure and right.

Proverbs 20:11

So then, Christian brothers, because of all this, be strong. Do not allow anyone to change your mind. Always do your work well for the Lord. You know that whatever you do for Him will not be wasted.

1 CORINTHIANS 15:58

Then your lives will please the Lord. You will do every kind of good work, and you will know more about God.

COLOSSIANS 1:10

Do your best to live a quiet life. Learn to do your own work well. We told you about this before. By doing this, you will be respected by those who are not Christians. Then you will not be in need and others will not have to help you.

1 THESSALONIANS 4:11–12

God always does what is right. He will not forget the work you did to help the Christians and the work you are still doing to help them. This shows your love for Christ. We want each one of you to keep on working to the end. Then what you hope for, will happen.

HEBREWS 6:10–11

Unless the Lord builds the house, its builders work for nothing. Unless the Lord watches over the city, the men who watch over it stay awake for nothing.

PSALM 127:1

Some good comes from all work. Nothing but talk leads only to being poor.

PROVERBS 14:23

WORRY

Do not worry. Learn to pray about everything. Give thanks to God as you ask Him for what you need. The peace of God is much greater than the human mind can understand. This peace will keep your hearts and minds through Christ Jesus.

PHILIPPIANS 4:6–7

God is our safe place and our strength. He is always our help when we are in trouble. So we will not be afraid, even if the earth is shaken and the mountains fall into the center of the sea, and even if its waters go wild with storm and the mountains shake with its action.

PSALM 46:1–3

And my God will give you everything you need because of His great riches in Christ Jesus.

PHILIPPIANS 4:19

"He will be like a tree planted by the water, that sends out its roots by the river. It will not be afraid when the heat comes but its leaves will be green. It will not be troubled in a dry year, or stop giving fruit."

JEREMIAH 17:8

Jesus said to her, "Martha, Martha, you are worried and troubled about many things. Only a few things are important, even just one. Mary has chosen the good thing. It will not be taken away from her."

LUKE 10:41–42

The Lord also keeps safe those who suffer. He is a safe place in times of trouble.

PSALM 9:9

You are my hiding place. You keep me safe from trouble. All around me are your songs of being made free.

PSALM 32:7

He will call upon Me, and I will answer him. I will be with him in trouble. I will take him out of trouble and honor him.

PSALM 91:15

We are pressed on every side, but we still have room to move. We are often in much trouble, but we never give up. People make it hard for us, but we are not left alone. We are knocked down, but we are not destroyed.

2 CORINTHIANS 4:8–9

We know that God makes all things work together for the good of those who love Him and are chosen to be a part of His plan.

ROMANS 8:28

The work of being right and good will give peace. From the right and good work will come quiet trust forever.

ISAIAH 32:17

"Do not worry. Do not keep saying, 'What will we eat?' or, 'What will we drink?' or, 'What will we wear?' The people who do not know God are looking for all these things. Your Father in heaven knows you need all these things."

MATTHEW 6:31–32

Give all your worries to Him because He cares for you.

1 PETER 5:7

"All the earth will worship You and sing praises to You. They will sing praises to Your name."

PSALM 66:4

Come, let us bow down in worship. Let us get down on our knees before the Lord Who made us. For He is our God. And we are the people of His field, and the sheep of His hand.

PSALM 95:6–7

Honor the Lord our God. And worship at His holy mountain. For the Lord our God is Holy!

PSALM 99:9

Jesus was born in the town of Bethlehem in the country of Judea. It was the time when Herod was king of that part of the country. Soon after Jesus was born, some wise men who learned things from stars came to Jerusalem from the East. They asked, "Where is the King of the Jews Who has been born?

We have seen His star in the East. We have come to worship Him."

MATTHEW 2:1–2

"God is Spirit. Those who worship Him must worship Him in spirit and in truth."

JOHN 4:24